WATER

by the same author

Geothermal Energy: *A Hot Prospect*
(published by Harcourt Brace Jovanovich)

Oceans of Energy: Reservoir of Power for the
Future
(published by Harcourt Brace Jovanovich)

Straight Hair, Curly Hair
(published by T. Y. Crowell)

The Bottom of the Sea
(published by T. Y. Crowell)

The Sunlit Sea
(published by T.Y. Crowell)

How to Release the Learning Power in Children
(published by Parker)

Grass: The Everything Everywhere Plant
(published by Thomas Nelson)

The Shape of Water
(published by Doubleday)

WATER

TOO MUCH, TOO LITTLE, TOO POLLUTED?

BY AUGUSTA GOLDIN

Illustrated with photographs and diagrams

Harcourt Brace Jovanovich, Publishers

San Diego   New York   London

All metric equivalents are approximate figures.

The author and publisher wish to thank the United Nations Development Programme for permission to reprint on page 16 the comment of the Nkobo girl from Southern Sudan; and Norman Longmate for using material from his book *King Cholera: The Biography of a Disease* on pages 55–56 and 131–134.

Designed by Mark Likgalter

Library of Congress Cataloging in Publication Data

Goldin, Augusta R.
  Water—too much, too little, too polluted?

  Bibliography: p.
  Includes index.
  Summary: Discusses the age-old quest for water all over the world; the hydrologic cycle; and obtaining fresh water from saline and atmospheric water as well as from underground and surface water.
  1. Water-supply—Juvenile literature. [1. Water supply] I. Title.
TD348.G64   1983   333.91   82-48760
ISBN 0-15-294819-8

First edition   B C D E
Printed in the United States of America

To all who inherit our water problems
and will need to know how to solve them

Contents

WATER

1

The First of Things Is Water

Water? Now here's a topic that has intrigued philosophers since time began. At first they merely talked and speculated about it. Later they wrote volumes of fiction and nonfiction about it. Then, about two thousand years ago, Pythagoras the Greek observed in one of his works:

> "The wise men of Miletus thus declared
> The first of things is water."

Surely those wise men were talking about usable, good-quality water, which, like air, is a necessity of life. Today we know that water is even more of a necessity than energy because we can always search out and substitute another form of energy for our use, but there is no substitute for water. Without water, plants and animals would soon become dehydrated and die. Without an *adequate* supply of usable water, civilization as we know it could not have developed because water not only supports life but also enriches it.

To the life of this planet, water is many things: It's

the mist rising in the valley, the rainbow in the sky, and a lacy cloud on a moonlit night. It's a spring bubbling in the desert, a driving rain, a blinding blizzard. As exploding steam, water generates electricity. As a glacier, it scrapes the countryside. To a child, water is a thirst quencher, but to a farmer, it's a promise of good harvests. Wars have been won because usable water was plentiful, and cities have been lost because it was not.

But is there enough water on this planet to support life magnificently for the four billion people that live here? Isn't it true, as the headlines scream, that we are suffering from droughts, vanishing supplies, and shortages?

It's true that in the last few years of the twentieth century there have been serious shortages. They have limited the production of vast agricultural regions and cut into a number of programs in mighty cities and great industrial complexes. In spite of such shortages, however, many experts see no cause for worry. They figure there's as much fresh water on the planet today as there ever was, even though the available amount computes to less than 1 percent of the world's estimated supply. (See the chart on page 5.) This amount, they note, is virtually fixed because water cannot be used up, nor can it be destroyed. It can only change in form, now being a liquid, now a solid, now a gas. Under given conditions these changes can go on endlessly.

When you heat water, it turns to vapor. The vapor adds humidity to the air, then condenses as droplets on walls and windows. When you freeze water in a tray, then place it on a sunny shelf, the ice melts and turns into water again. Outdoors, in sub-zero weather, those same ice cubes would sublimate—that is, change from the frozen state to vapor. Even when you pour water down the drain, it eventually finds its way to the ocean. It is not lost; neither is the amount diminished.

Another wonder inherent in the nature of water is that it is a permanent resource.

Consider the fact that water may be locked up in great glaciers for centuries. This water isn't lost. It's only temporarily unavailable because it's in a solid state.

Or consider the fact that water cannot boil out of the oceans, the reason being that water is never static. The slightest rise in temperature makes the water molecules circulate faster. Watch a potful of water heating on the stove. The hotter it gets, the more active the water becomes. If you move a candy thermometer around in that pot, you'll find that every part of the liquid is equally heated. The same thing happens outdoors in a roadside puddle. Under the noonday sun, as the temperature rises, the water molecules circulate faster. They may circulate so fast that they zip out of the puddle and evaporate altogether. On a larger scale, this kind of circulation also goes on in the ocean. But because the oceans are all interlocked and their waters intermingle, it would be impossible for the water to reach the boiling point, even at the equator, as long as the poles are covered with glaciers. According to the Russian authority M. I. Luvovich, author of *The World's Water*, every drop in the world ocean is completely mixed or replaced every sixty-three years.

Consider this fact, too: although water evaporates, it cannot escape from the planet and float off into space. As invisible vapor, it constantly rises from the land and sea until it reaches a level where the atmosphere is thinner and the pressure reduced. There the vapor expands, and, as it expands, it cools. Now cool air cannot hold as much moisture as warm air, so heavy droplets begin to form. Indeed, you can see this sort of thing happening when you open your bathroom door after you've taken a hot

DISTRIBUTION OF WORLD'S ESTIMATED WATER SUPPLY

Location	Surface area (square miles)	Water volume (cubic miles)*	Percentage of total water
SURFACE WATER			
Fresh-water lakes	330,000	30,000	.009
Saline lakes and inland seas	270,000	25,000	.008
Average in stream channels	—	300	.0001
SUBSURFACE WATER			
Vadose water (includes soil moisture)		16,000	.005
Ground water within depth of half a mile	50,000,000	1,000,000	.31
Ground water— deep lying		1,000,000	.31
OTHER WATER LOCATIONS			
Icecaps and glaciers	6,900,000	7,000,000	2.15
Atmosphere (at sea level)	197,000,000	3,100	.001
World ocean	139,500,000	317,000,000	97.2
TOTALS(rounded)	—	326,000,000	100

* One cubic mile of water equals 1.1 trillion gallons.

U.S. Department of the Interior/Geological Survey

Of the world's water supply, only some .6341 percent is fresh and found in fresh-water lakes, in streams and channels, in vadose form (just below the surface and in the soil), and under the ground to a depth of one mile. The water locked up in glaciers is not available. (U.S. Department of the Interior/Geological Survey) shower. With the door open, the saturated air is cooled. Then droplets of water form on the steamed-up mirror and begin to run down. In less than an hour, though, the mirror will be dry again. The droplets will be gone, having evaporated and changed back to invisible vapor and, once again, become part of the air.

In the upper atmosphere, these droplets form around particles of wind-blown dust or salt spray creating clouds. Under suitable conditions these drops may fall as rain or

An abandoned farm near Boardman, Oregon, that has been devastated by dust storms. (USDA—Soil Conservation Service)

Silting caused by flooding in Lancaster, Texas. (USDA—Soil Conservation Service photo by John McConnell)

hail, sleet or snow. Vapor that doesn't condense may continue to rise, but it eventually reaches the cut-off point in temperature beyond which it cannot rise. Then it, too, condenses into droplets.

Although fresh water in its many forms is a permanent and renewable resource that clearly cannot be diminished, the supply here and there may be so erratic that it sometimes seems as if the world really is running short. Occasionally prolonged droughts and dust storms whirl for hundreds of miles, burying fields and fences, houses and barns. Even torrential rains can create a shortage of fresh water. When water rises and goes on a rampage, it washes out thousands of fields and covers others with mud. It's a fact that communities stricken by drought and dying of thirst one year may be destroyed by flood waters the next. In either instance, the people face a shortage of usable water. In addition, there are increasingly polluted waterways, lowered ground-water levels, and eroded watersheds. There are also new and congested urban developments demanding more and more water. Not surprisingly, irrigation pipes and municipal reservoirs begin to run dry, and the media announce a water shortage, calling it an act of God. In this book, such shortages will be referred to as *mismanagement of the supply*, meaning that the water supply had been taken for granted, overdrawn, and abused by contaminants. Under such conditions, mismanagement of the supply becomes synonomous with ecological malpractice.

In early times, man's search for fresh water was simple. Wherever surface water existed, it was easily located: a tumbling stream here, a quiet pond there, or a trickle of drops down a hillside. But because man always liked sunshine and dry weather, he often chose to live in semiarid areas. If the water was scarce or of poor quality, he had to make a choice. Barefoot, and using a stone-chipped hoe, he would scoop out a small hole in the sand or hack out a shallow well in the rock and wait for it to fill with water. Or he would pile stones in an ankle-deep brook, dam it up, and have a pool. If that wasn't enough, he could search for water farther away, then move his family to it or have his wife carry it to their family.

Transporting water became a big job that required community collaboration when more water was needed or wanted because the population had increased or the standard of living had improved. Then clear regulations had to be spelled out concerning the control and use of the water.

One of the earliest examples of community collaboration to provide water for the people was Jacob's Well. The Bible tells that this 105-foot (32-meter) well was sunk through solid rock some four thousand years ago. And earlier ruins, in the Indus Valley, tell of a community water supply with such modern features as drainage systems, swimming pools and baths, tanks, and irrigation canals. Similar facilities were also enjoyed by the Babylonians, the Greeks, the Romans, the Egyptians, and the

Chinese, while the Egyptians, using slave labor, constructed the first known dam to hold back the spring floods and store water for irrigation.

Throughout history, water, even more than land, shaped the social behavior of man. Land was everywhere, but fresh water, except in the rain forests and along the riverbanks, had to be searched for. It's not surprising that the ancient religions describe so feelingly the aspirations of the desert tribes as they wandered with their flocks, searching for water.

Read Psalms 104:10-11: "He sendeth the springs into the valleys, which run among the hills. They give drink to every beast in the field; the wild asses quench their thirst."

Ponder Deuteronomy 8:7: "For the Lord thy God bringeth thee into a good land, a land of brooks of water, of fountains and depths that spring out of valleys and hills. . . ."

Consider the appreciation expressed in Psalms 78:15-16: "He clave the rocks in the wilderness and gave them drink out of great depths. He brought streams also out of the rock and caused water to run like rivers."

Because water has always been so precious, water rights actually antedate land ownership. Ancient writings show how the possession of a water source was protected morally and legally. For example, a man could not own his land unless he had first dug a well to provide water for that land. In Persia and Palestine, these wells were constructed without curbings, and their location was kept secret so that roving tribes couldn't steal the water for their flocks.

Among the Moslems, who believed that "no man can refuse water without sinning against Allah and man," an enemy in need of water was first allowed to slake his thirst, then treated as an enemy.

In what is now Latin America, northern Europe, and that great arc of land stretching from Egypt to India and

China, the ancients frequently used water in their religious ceremonies. The Catholic Church, too, shortly after its establishment, directed the priests to sanctify the water used in their services. And because Jesus was baptized in the Jordan River, thousands still journey to the Jordan for bottles of this holy water, with which they baptize their children back home. Similarly, devout Hindus make pilgrimages to bathe in the Ganges River.

Even marriage customs have been tied in historically with the need for good water. In some communities in southwest Asia, where the nearest source of water was 7, 8, or 9 miles (11 to 14 kilometers) distant, wives were invariably the water-fetchers. Jugs balanced on their heads, even the youngest and fleetest of these barefoot women could make only one trip a day. Multiple wives then became a necessity, as well as a mark of affluence. In most parts of Africa, Asia, and Latin America, women and children are still the primary water-fetchers. Only in China do men carry water to the home.

As communities grew larger and the management of water resources became more involved, traditional practices gave way to codified law. The first known lawgiver was Hammurabi, King of the Babylonians in the eighteenth century B.C., remembered for his statutes regarding the building, use, and maintenance of their irrigation canals. About 1,200 years later, in the sixth century B.C., the famous Greek lawgiver Solon developed additional statutes, which encouraged the use and control of the water supply as it related to familial needs. Accordingly, water was to be free and available to all who lived within .5 mile (.8 kilometer) from a public well. Beyond that distance, each family was required to dig its own well, at least 6 feet (2 meters) from his neighbor's boundary line. However, up to 12 gallons (45 liters) of water a day was to be given freely to the more distant inhabitants if they had already dug down 60 feet (18 meters) but failed to reach water.

*   *   *

For long millenniums, water regulations referred only to the fresh water needed by people for themselves, their domesticated animals, and their irrigated fields. In the thirteenth century, after the Crusaders returned from the Holy Land, trade began to quicken. In England the traders began agitating for free use of inland waterways. At that time, free use of the waterways for commercial purposes was an altogether new concept. But because it would mean better business, all tolls and barriers were removed, and free use was granted by King John. This was such an important decision that it was written into the Magna Carta, signed at Runnymede in 1215.

More important than the free use, however, was the preservation of clean and unpolluted waterways so that the water could be used again and again by the people along the banks. Long before the Magna Carta was written, rules for maintaining waterways had already been established in many parts of the world. Starting at the head of streams and canals, all users were required to participate in the cleanup and to consume no more than their allotted share of water. Those early users didn't know how the cleanups kept the water fresh in the rivers, lakes, and canals. They only knew that when watercourses became laden with refuse, with salt and/or silt, the fish and the familiar water plants died. Then the water became stagnant, smelled bad, and turned into a foul and evil-tasting brew.

Today, this description fits many of our waterways because the users have not been effectively required to participate in the cleanups. The Ohio, the Mississippi, the Danube, and the Ganges are now heavily polluted, as are also some areas around the Great Lakes and such inland seas as the Black and the Mediterranean. These waters are impaired for use because they are polluted with organic runoff from farm fields and with municipal wastes. Some are also polluted with radioactive and thermal wastes from certain industrial projects. Many of these contaminants boost the growth of algae, which quickly blanket the water. In short order, then, these algae consume the oxygen in the water. The marine plants and animals suffocate, decay, and begin to stink—a process called *eutrophication*. Consequently, the rivers become running sewers, while the lakes and inland seas simply store the noxious wastes that drain into them.

When watercourses are used as sewers, the water becomes unfit for drinking, for irrigation, or for industrial use. The result is a fresh-water shortage—a shortage in the midst of brimming lakes and running rivers.

Scientists are only now discovering what those early long-haired, sun-browned farmers knew centuries ago— that rivers and lakes can cleanse themselves unless they are overwhelmed by pollutants. A bit of pollution here and there doesn't matter too much because enough oxygen can be absorbed by the running rivers and wind-tossed lake waters to support aquatic life. The fish and other animals can then feed on the thriving water plants, and in due time the ever present bacteria consume the animal residues. Under such conditions, river and lake waters run clear and sparkling and fresh. In this way, water continues to be a renewable resource that is fresh and *potable*—that is, looks good, smells good, tastes good, and is free of an undue amount of harmful contaminants.

The age-old search for a steady supply of good-quality water and the all-too-customary mismanagement of that supply are two sides of the same coin. Under mismanagement, when a city's water supply becomes unusable and the cost of chemical treatment becomes too painful, the order goes out to search for new sources, no matter how distant. Under mismanagement, when the supply is overdrawn (as it is in some agricultural areas that depend on irrigation), the search goes deeper. Then weather-beaten farmers, tired of scanning the hot blue sky for rain clouds, sink their wells deeper, until nature's counter-effects become evident. The underground water levels may then drop drastically—as much as 10 feet (3 meters) a year, as has happened in Texas and Arizona. Then the land may develop huge fissures, building foundations may crack, houses may sink, and roadways may buckle. When wells are of necessity drilled still deeper, brine instead of fresh water often flows from the underground source. In other places, sink holes may develop, as has happened in Florida.

This fissure near Apache Junction, Arizona, is believed to have been caused by the excessive withdrawal of ground water. (U.S. Department of the Interior, Bureau of Reclamation photo by E. E. Hertzog)

This sink hole in Winter Park, Florida, is 40 feet (12.2 meters) deep— down to the lowered water level. (Florida Bureau of Geology, photo by Rich Deuerling, May 1981)

As we near the twenty-first century, scientists, economists, and farmers are beginning to realize that the key to survival is water that is usable, safe, and available. And there is increasing talk about the urgent need for cooperative policy-planning on regional, national, and international levels.

Now, cooperative policy planning, especially on the international level, is slow. There are language barriers and cultural differences. There are economic problems and shifting political alliances. Even when large-scale conferences are arranged, progress is slow. Of the several that were set up in the second half of the twentieth century, the one that was perhaps the most meaningful was the 1967 Water for Peace Conference. It was suggested by President Lyndon B. Johnson, who called attention to the fact that famines, which periodically decimate the populations in many Third World countries, are caused by crop failures, which in turn are caused by the lack of a reliable water supply. He made it clear that what was needed in those famine-stricken countries was not yet another handout, but water—water for that starving world.

This conference, like all the others, ended with some great recommendations, but since those recommendations were nonbinding, nothing much came of them.

Now mark the year 1980—the year when the United Nations mounted its International Drinking Water Supply and Sanitation Decade. On November 10, Bradford Morse, Administrator of the United Nations Development Programme (UNDP), rose to speak at a special session of the General Assembly. "What angers me," he said, "is the simple fact that if water were oil, we would have many times the financial commitment expressed to date for this Decade, and many times the number of journalists attending this session. We are willing to invest vastly more in ensuring enough gas for our automobiles than we have been in assuring the minimum basic standards of good health and productivity for the world's poor. We are eager to pay for petro, but not for the safe water which is essential to life itself."

Bradford Morse was referring to the Third World: to the 30,000 graves that are dug every day for those who die because of contaminated water and inadequate sanitation facilities; to the one child in every two who, felled by diseases related to contaminated water or to contact with excreta, never reaches age five in certain areas.

Throughout Launch Day, mention was made of the fact that 2 billion people—half of the world's population— do not have easy access to potable water or to adequate waste-disposal facilities. In the developing countries, according to the UNDP, this computes, on the average, to three out of five people drinking contaminated water and three out of four using the bush and the open fields to relieve themselves.

> "Water? Where do I get it? Oh, I walk two hours every time and two hours back. I do this twice a day. . . . Are we sick? Oh, often we have running stomachs, especially my small brothers and sisters. If only we could get a well in the village . . ."
>
> Nkobo girl
> Southern Sudan

By the early 1980s village wells were still scarce in the Third World. People had to make do with the limited quantities the women and children could carry home. Consequently, they never had enough for drinking, cooking, washing and bathing, laundering clothes, scrubbing floors, and certainly none left over for sprinkling the garden. The result was widespread disease and low agricultural production, which leads to poverty, malnutrition, and high mortality rates among children. It was this condition that the UN aimed to improve.

Women in Upper Volta walk many hours a day carrying water from a distant source to their homes. (UNICEF photo by Pierre Wolf)

In 1981 UNICEF spent $50.6 million to help ninety-three countries meet the objective of providing a constant supply of safe water at a convenient distance from home. UNICEF also promoted a program of breast-feeding. Barefoot doctors were sent from village to village to point out that the use of unsterilized bottles and unsafe water mixed with the baby formula was what was killing off thousands of infants every year.

In 1982, the World Bank and related UN agencies sponsored the Rural Water Supply Handpumps Project. The aim was to provide one and a half billion people in the developing countries of Asia, Africa, and Latin America with six or seven million handpumps by the year 1990. The rationale behind this project was that wherever good-quality ground water was available, it could be lifted to the surface most economically by handpumps.

Throughout the water decade, UN scientific teams will be cooperating with the Third World communities that need help in order to obtain the water they need. But the story doesn't end here because the level of consciousness is rising rapidly, especially among the women. A case in point can be found in Kenya. There, in a determined effort to free themselves from the endless drudgery of walking six or seven hours a day to and from distant water sources, the young mothers organized themselves into groups. Then, by their own labor, these women with babies on their backs and in their wombs dug miles of trenches. They laid the waterpipes and brought good water from the far mountains to standpipes in their villages. (See the photograph on page 18.)

Around the world, the search for usable water that is available, abundant, and safe is gaining momentum. In the developing countries this search is sparked by the people's dire need. It is propelled by their physical labor and directed by the development of appropriate technology that suits their environment and their economy.

Mothers digging a trench for a community water supply project in Kenya. (Camerapix/Earthscan. Reprinted by courtesy of World Water *magazine)*

In the industrialized countries, the search is backed by sophisticated power-driven technology including remote sensing devices and geophysical techniques. Today and for years to come we can expect to find water prospectors, agricultural engineers, and related scientists engaging in a quest:

• to locate unsuspected water sources under the ground: geothermal water, heated by masses of molten rock in the earth's depth, and fossil ground water stored during the rainy periods of the Ice Age;

• to capture additional supplies of water from the atmosphere by short-circuiting the hydrologic cycle, that is, by steering rain clouds to designated areas and inducing them to release their moisture;

• to explore economical ways to desalinate seawater;

• to divert the flow of rivers in order to bring fresh water to areas that need it.

We can also expect to see farmers concerning themselves with the retention of soil moisture that's generally lost to evaporation; and botanists developing drought-resistant plants that require very little fresh water, and salt-tolerant plants that can thrive on the briny deposits that underlie many desert areas.

Additionally, we can expect to see engineers who specialize in environmental science designing ever more effective methods for reusing and reclaiming water that would otherwise have been wasted to the sewers and/or the nearest rivers.

We are talking about a multifaceted global search that will require the cooperation of hydrologists, chemists, biologists, engineers, economists, geologists, and environmentalists, as well as farmers, legislators, medical specialists, and an informed public. This search will unquestionably lead to the development of new sources that may someday be commonplace. In the meantime, better management of the water already available will solve most of our so-called shortages. That is as it should be because, as the wise men of Miletus declared, "The first of things is water."

The story of civilization has always been interwoven with the search for fresh-water supplies that are safe and conveniently accessible. Now, with the exploding global population using ever more water, it is necessary to learn how to utilize the supplies efficiently. For us, in this technological age, the search and the learning are urgent. How this urgency will propel our twentieth-century water programs into the twenty-first century is what this book is about.

2

The Age-Old Quest for Water

In these last decades of the twentieth century, the water have-nots in the developing countries of Asia, Africa, and Latin America pose a problem that concerns the world. Without sufficient potable water, these people cannot maintain an adequate level of personal hygiene and good health. Being undernourished and sickly, they cannot raise enough food to feed themselves, let alone to trade. For them, Western handouts of bulging sacks of seed and fertilizer will not solve the problem because great crops will not grow where farmers are too enfeebled to cultivate their semiarid lands effectively. For these people the answer lies in potable water: in finding and developing adequate sources of it, in treating it, in transporting it, and in distributing it economically.

This need for potable water is not a new phenomenon. It was every bit as urgent in the old days, before man even knew he was man. In those long-ago days, man managed instinctively. He followed the wild beasts and drank where they drank—from lakes, streams, springs, water holes, and puddles. And like the wild beasts, when the familiar supplies dried up, he would scramble about in parched stream beds looking for small, temporary water holes where he could slake his thirst.

Throughout the millenniums, as long as the population was sparse—a family here, a tribe there—the surface waters sufficed for the human wanderers. Then, about ten thousand years ago, after the last Ice Age ended, the climate became milder. Great changes began to take place in what is now called the Fertile Crescent and the Cradle of Civilization. In those dry, sunny lands of Egypt, the Middle East, and Persia (now Iran), as well as in parts of India and China, the people learned to domesticate animals. They became herders. They took to raising thousands of woolly sheep and driving them across the desert from one water hole to another. Behind the sheep plodded the many wives and their lively children, followed by the snorting camels with folded black tents strapped to their backs. And bringing up the rear were the skittish long-eared goats that provided milk and butter and cheese.

About eight thousand years ago, some of the herders

learned that it really wasn't necessary constantly to trek those hundreds of miles for water because there was plenty of it underground. They had only to deepen a spring or dig into a damp meadow and they'd get a shallow well brimming with water. So some settled down and became farmers, and some established themselves in small hamlets, which, in time, grew into thriving towns bustling with craftsmen and peddlers, traders, merchants, priests, and even schoolteachers (for boys only). But as the towns grew, so did the need for water. Naturally, the townspeople envied the herders in the desert because they could always follow the well-known water routes. And just as naturally, they envied the farmers, who could rely on the mighty rivers (the Nile, the Tigris and Euphrates, the Yellow, and the Indus) to flood their fields every spring and enrich them with a coating of silt. For thirsty townspeople, a faraway water hole or a river cresting in the spring was not much good. Still, because they had enterprising leaders, they managed to get the water they needed, and so they thrived. They constructed canals that brought distant mountain water to the cities for public use. And the householders, together with their muscular sons, dug their own wells in their own backyards, becoming quite expert. They learned that a hole 3 feet (1 meter) wide and 10, 20, or 30 feet (3, 6, or 9 meters) deep, if sited in a likely place, would usually fill with enough water to supply their needs. They also learned that if they lined the hole with boards or logs or fieldstones this would keep the sides from caving in and muddying the supply.

But still the towns continued to grow, and the burghers soon found that the canals simply did not deliver enough water to keep the public businesses going. It became clear that public wells that were much wider and much deeper were needed.

In town square after town square, long-bearded patriarchs and prophets and seers began conferring endlessly, asking themselves: Where shall we locate our wells? How deep will we have to dig? Can we be sure that we'll strike good water?

Although these were bothersome questions to which no one had the answers, they had to be asked because the need for a dependable and abundant water supply was too acute. If water could not be found on the surface or in nearby springs, they would have to go underground for it. As for labor, nobody worried about that because labor was cheap. Didn't every man have two hands and a strong back? And if more help was needed, they could always raid a nearby settlement or two and capture a few hundred slaves.

Actually, historical records show that long before the Christian era, deep-well technology in the Middle and Far East was already quite sophisticated. For excavating through sand and gravel, well-diggers used picks and shovel-like tools. As for the debris that accumulated in the *bore*, or hole, historians believe it was probably hauled up in buckets with a windlass. (A windlass is a device that's shaped like a horizontal spool on which the lifting rope winds.) For digging through solid rock, they used another method as simple as it was ingenious. The men drilled small holes in the rock with crude augurs, then pounded wooden pegs into the holes, and flooded the pegs with water. The pegs would absorb the water, swell up, and crack the rock as neatly as any power tools in use today.

These wells were very large, and, once dug, they began to fill with water. So far, so good. But now another problem presented itself: in these deep wells the water rose only half or three-quarters of the way to the top. In some, it rose only a quarter of the way. How to get the water to the surface with a minimum of effort was the question.

Of course, the people knew about water-lifting devices and had long used them in their shallow wells. A bucket at the end of a rope enabled even a small child to haul up a drink for himself, his mother, or his faithful dog. This was such a handy system that in those days no traveler ever left home without a coil of rope and a bucket so that he could help himself to water when he chanced upon a well.

Another device was the pole with a bucket attached to the end that was lowered into the well. A push on the pole made the bucket turn over and quickly fill up with water. There was also the well sweep, which consisted of a long pole (the sweep), a short rope, a bucket, and a deeply notched 10-foot (3-meter) stump set into the ground near the well. The middle of the sweep was secured to the notched stump, and into the well went one end of the sweep, with the bucket dangling from it. Whoever wanted some water had only to lift and lower the free end of the sweep and a cold, sparkling bucketful would come sloshing up from the well.

Other householders favored the windlass to lift water out of the well. The windlass has never gone out of style. You can still see one occasionally on some farm or other in almost every country in the world.

But when the really deep wells—more than 100 feet (30 meters) deep—were constructed, other water-lifting devices had to be contrived. In *The Story of Man's Search for Water*, Jasper Owen Draffin, former professor of theoretical and applied mechanics at the University of Illinois, said, "Some of the ancient wells had steps on the inside by means of which a person descended and, after filling the jar, returned to the surface. This method of obtaining water is suggested in the case of the servant of Abraham who went in search of a wife for the young man Isaac. It will be recalled that Rebekah 'went down to the well, and filled her pitcher, and came up' (Genesis 24:16). Incidentally, the occasion throws light on the customs and spirit of the times when a man allowed a young girl to draw sufficient water for ten camels—and camels are not small drinkers in a hot and arid region."

As might be expected, more efficient water-lifting devices were invented in time. One used in India consisted of a leather bag, called a *mote*, suspended inside the well by a rope. The other end of the rope was threaded through a pulley and hitched to a pair of bullocks. It was the job of the bullocks to raise and lower the mote, and believe it or not, they did just that and brought up anywhere from 800 to 2,000 gallons (3,028 to 7,561 liters) of water an hour.

One of the many ancient devices that can still be seen churning away in some parts of Egypt and southern Asia is the Persian water wheel, which was used by the Moguls. According to George C. Taylor, Jr., formerly of

A Persian water wheel is powered by a bullock in India. (FAO photo by T. S. Satyan)

the United States Geological Survey (USGS), "It consists of an endless chain of earthen pots or small metal buckets that are passed over a wheel with a horizontal axis. A camel or a pair of bullocks pushes a horizontal bar around a vertical shaft geared to a wheel and thus raises the water in the pots. Because of its greater efficiency, a water wheel can lift greater quantities of water than a pair of bullocks and a mote." In some areas, a Persian water wheel is powered by a man's legs.

As well technology and water-lifting devices improved, deeper wells were dug not only to serve the cities but also to make life easier and more pleasant for the military, the royalty, and the religious, wherever they might be located. In Lahore and Srinagar, in the provinces of Punjab and Kashmir, deep wells provided a plenitude of water for the Indian troops stationed on the British frontier. At many Hindu temples, wells 50 to 100 feet (15 to 30 meters) in diameter were dug down to the water source so the religious could perform their ritual ablutions while sitting on the *ghats* (steps) that bordered them.

And the palace wells! These, especially in Persia, were really fit for royalty. Reaching down as much as 300 feet (90 meters), they had lavishly decorated walls inlaid with blue and green glazed mosaics and white marble panels.

Most of those wells have since fallen into disrepair and been lost in antiquity, but there are some that history will not let us forget. Two are especially remembered for their holiness. One is Jacob's Well because it was there that Jesus talked with the women of Samaria when they came to fill their water jugs. Without doubt, this well must have been constructed with augurs and wooden pegs because, lacking modern technology, there was no other way that the men of Palestine could have excavated 105 feet (31 meters)—a depth equivalent to ten or twelve stories—through solid rock.

Another famous well is the Zemzem Well in Mecca,

which the Mohammedans consider the holiest in the world because it was Zemzem water that sustained Ishmael in the wilderness so that he was able to go on and become the progenitor of the Arabs.

Wherever there were noted centers of industry, art, and religion, you can be sure that the people had dug the necessary wells. You can also be sure that, politics permitting, even more water was often provided by canals bringing water from the hillside springs and the upper reaches of some rivers. This water was, of course, used for domestic purposes, but not always. At times, some of the canal water would be diverted for irrigating distant farm fields or for constructing pleasure projects for the kings and their families.

One great project was undertaken by the Assyrian King Sennacherib, who lived in the seventh century B.C. and was one of the world's first environmentalists. He made up his mind to bring fresh water—and lots of it—from the faraway hills to his capital city of Nineveh, as well as to the surrounding farmlands, because he loved to be surrounded by luxuriant orchards. He therefore decreed that a 50-mile (80-kilometer) canal be constructed. Abundant water was then provided to the surrounding fields, as well as to the city's official buildings and temples and palaces, to the government armory, and to the king's special parks and gardens, which soon became famous for two reasons: they were adorned with hundreds of splashing fountains, and they were magnificently stocked with plants and animals imported from distant countries.

Perhaps the most famous of the pleasure projects was the Hanging Gardens of Babylon, which became known as one of the Seven Wonders of the World. These gardens were constructed in the sixth century B.C. by King Nebuchadnezzar II, who, according to legend, thought they would make his wife, a former mountain princess, feel more at home in the Mesopotamian desert. And to keep those gardens green and growing and well irrigated, he had legions of slaves turning huge Archimedes screws to lift the water from the Euphrates River.

Of course, Assyrians and Babylonians weren't the only peoples to build canals and watercourses. In their quest for more and more water, the Greeks and the Phoenicians did the same thing.

But the greatest watercourse designers of all time were the Romans, who built their aqueducts to last. The word aqueduct, which comes from the Latin *aqua*, meaning water, and *ducere*, meaning to lead, immediately makes one think of those great tiers of arches that brought water to Rome. Actually, the arches are only the supports for the aqueduct, which is a combination of canals, tunnels, and pipes.

In building their aqueducts, the ancient Roman engineers used canals and tunnels and pipes because they knew a thing or two about water pressure. They knew that in order to get water safely and consistently down from the distant mountain springs, they had to control the rate of descent and keep the flow even. Without such control, the surging water would rush down those steep declines and build up so much pressure that the pipes and the tunnels would burst. So down the graded mountainsides they ran their brick-lined canals, and through the highest mountains they drove their massive tunnels, blasting the rocks with fire and cold water. Across the deep valleys they erected tier upon tier of stone arches to carry the great pipes: some made of hollowed-out logs, most of lead. And always, with an eye on their surveying instruments, the engineers checked the gradient and the rate of flow. When all the construction was complete and all the controls were operating, the mountain waters were allowed to fill the canals, tunnels, and pipes and finally to splash into Rome's reservoirs, cisterns, pools, bathhouses, and marble fountains, 30, 40, or 50 miles (50, 65, or 80 kilometers) away.

Aqua Appia, begun in 312 B.C., was the first of the aqueducts to bring water to Rome. How pleased the citizens were to get such an abundant supply of fresh water. Little did they know that this fresh water was not exactly potable. The lead pipes that brought the water also brought the possibility of lead poisoning to the populace, but this knowledge was still far in the future. Today some antiquarians suggest that Rome's later downfall may have been due, in part, to centuries of lead poisoning, with its attendant effect on the physical and mental health of the people.

But some aqueducts are still operating. Others are in a state of disrepair but still standing. One ancient aqueduct, 16 miles (26 kilometers) in length started by Hadrian in 134 A.D., has operated without a break except for a brief period in 1926, when it was repaired and enlarged. That's about eighteen and a half centuries of operation! Of the eleven aqueducts that were constructed in the third century A.D., four, also rebuilt, are still functioning, bringing water from mountains that are 50 miles (80 kilometers) distant.

To map the construction of aqueducts across Europe is to trace the advancing Roman legions as they conquered one country after another. In Nîmes, France, you

The Pont du Gard, near Nîmes, France. (From T. Schreiber, Atlas of Classical Antiquities, *1895)*

can see the famous remains of the Pont du Gard that was constructed in the time of Jesus. Although now dry and inoperable, it still spans the river on three tiers of stone arches that measure 855 feet (261 meters) in length and 155 feet (47 meters) in height—a constant reminder of unbeatable Roman engineering. Also, far away in Segovia, Spain, they built one that, running over a double tier of arches, still brings water to the city.

Prior to the Dark Ages, which began with the fall of Rome in 476 A.D., man's age-old quest for water had taken three directions:
- He searched for surface sources of water.
- He searched for underground sources of water.
- He searched for ever better ways to transport that water from distant sources to his point of need—to cities and farm fields.

Although the conduction of water had reached a high level of efficiency with the Romans, it was, in the main, an overland system. However, yet another form of water transport, an underground system, was so highly developed for irrigation in the mid-Asian and north African deserts that it supported great civilizations millenniums ago. This system is known as the *karez (kharez)* in Afghanistan, the *ghanat* in Iran, the *falaj* in Oman, and the *fogarra* in the Sahara.

In olden days these underground systems were blue-printed, so to speak, by the elders who were wise in the ways of water. They would go to the mountains, study the terrain, and dig here and there until they struck the *water table.* By definition the water table is the upper limit of the underlying layer of saturated earth and rock. Understandably, the depth at which the table occurs varies. It's closer to the surface in regions of great rainfall, deeper down where rain is scarce.

When those ancients dug down to the water table, as often as not they found that they had constructed a well that was 20 or 30 feet (6 or 9 meters) deep or even as much as 650 feet (198 meters). Naturally, the water rose in the well, but only to a depth of a foot or two because they had merely tapped into the water table for a short distance since that was all they wanted at that time. They then dug another well near the first one, which they called the Mother Well, and studied the slope of the land, trying to figure out at what point downslope the water table would be most likely to come closest to the surface. After that, without the help of any surveying instruments, they cleverly dug a tunnel from the bottom of the well, along the natural slope of the water table, to the place where it approached the surface, and the well water would drain from the well, through the tunnel, to the surface outlet, sometimes at a brisk 2 cubic feet (.6 cubic meter) per second, and provide the community with a reliable supply of irrigation and household water.

All this sounds simple, doesn't it? According to George Taylor, however, karez construction was back-breaking work and very dangerous. "Imagine," he says, "climbing down into a well that may have been fifty or sixty stories deep, and starting to dig there, in the wet darkness. Imagine crouching inside those tunnels that were seldom more than about 4 feet [1.2 meters] high." Besides the cramping bodily discomfort and the chance of being carried off by pneumonia or crushed by collapsing ceilings, the immediate problem was the excavated debris. What were they to do with it? Well, the ancients hoisted it up through vertical shafts that extended from the water tables to the surface. These shafts were spaced at intervals ranging from 20 to 100 feet (6 to 30 meters). In some parts of mid Asia, shaft openings that from the air look like small bomb craters can still be seen punctuating the desert. Men are still periodically sent down into them to clean out the tunnels so the water can continue to flow freely.

Of course, nobody in his right mind ever volunteered for these jobs. Nobody wanted to be a digger despite such inducements as higher pay and extra wives. But the kings in those days knew that their desert civilization depended on water. They knew that these underground irrigation systems were absolutely essential if the fields were to be kept productive. And so, according to legend, a decree went forth: Karez diggers and their sons and their sons' sons were to serve in those tunnels for life. You may be sure, however, that for most of them, life in those wet, black, caving-in tunnels was short.

Karezes, ghanats, falajes, and fogarras were constructed by the hundreds, for miles on end, often crisscrossing each other at various levels under the Asian and African deserts. Many are still operative and kept in good repair. In fact, some Iranian ghanats that were constructed about three thousand years ago are still serving the women of Khuzistan, who gather at the outlets every morning to draw their daily ration of household water. Nor have conditions changed much in the nearby countries.

A study in Afghanistan, conducted in the early 1970s by a USGS mission, found some eighty karezes in the Zamin Dawar area that are still providing the water necessary for domestic use, for running water mills and irrigating farm fields, and for raising cattle, horses, and camels. Geologist Neal E. McClymonds, author of the mission's report, states that just like the ancient ones, most of today's tunnels are unlined, although caving sections are usually shored up by baked clay rings that resemble horse collars. He also notes that the mother wells he observed had generally been dug 6 to 16 feet (2 to 5 meters) below the water table and that the tunnels, too, had been dug below the water table for the first 330 to 990 feet (100 to 320 meters), after which they ran laterally above the water table. Says McClymonds, "In essence, this layout makes a karez a horizontal well." (See the diagram on page 33.)

The karezes described above are relatively new, although they are older than the oldest memories of the oldest villagers, which would compute to about 300 years.

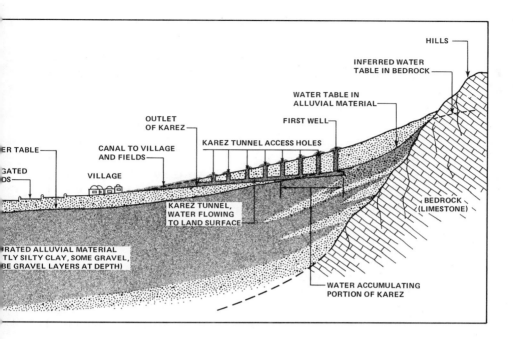

HILLS

INFERRED WATER
TABLE IN BEDROCK

WATER TABLE IN
ALLUVIAL MATERIAL

OUTLET
OF KAREZ

FIRST WELL

CANAL TO VILLAGE
AND FIELDS

KAREZ TUNNEL ACCESS HOLES

ER TABLE

GATED
DS

VILLAGE

BEDROCK
(LIMESTONE)

KAREZ TUNNEL,
WATER FLOWING
TO LAND SURFACE

RATED ALLUVIAL MATERIAL
TLY SILTY CLAY, SOME GRAVEL,
BE GRAVEL LAYERS AT DEPTH)

WATER ACCUMULATING
PORTION OF KAREZ

*A generalized cross-section of a karez and its method of operation.
(U.S. Geological Survey, after McClymonds, 1972)*

Here, the peasants share the flowing water according to
the number of *jiribs* each owns. (A jirib is equivalent to 2
acres, or .8 hectare.) Of necessity, the water code is very
strict.

At this point you must be wondering why, for all
those thousands of years, those millions of people had
bothered with underground transport systems instead of
developing aboveground transport systems. Actually, in
those searing deserts, they had no choice. Canals would
do them little good because the hot sun would evaporate
much of the running water, or sand storms would bury
the canals altogether. So it was karezes or nothing. The
people chose underground systems because of the abundance of underground water, and in this way they kept
their civilization going. As James R. Jones, the leader of

that USGS team in Afghanistan, told this author, "To this day, much of the irrigated land in western Asia depends on the karezes. And there's still plenty of water under the ground."

Asked why those reserves hadn't been exhausted by long millenniums of use, Jones explained, "With their primitive engineering methods, the Afghans had had no way of overdrawing the supply. All they could withdraw was what flowed naturally from the outlet. If they'd had the technology we have today—diesel engines and turbines and electric pumps—they would have drained those desert aquifers dry ages ago just as we have done in the American Southwest."

Wherever desert conditions existed, innovative irrigation schemes have always been devised to move the surface water or to get the water out of the ground. A case in point is Libya, that new, independent, oil-rich, water-poor country. Today, scientific teams are searching for and developing her ground-water reserves, but there was a time, long, long ago, when things were different. Then the *surface* waters were sufficient to support her great populations.

When the Romans came, they engineered aqueducts that brought water from the distant hill springs to the city bathhouses and marble fountains. Later, the Arabs constructed horizontal wells (here called fogarras) that carried water to the fields. Still later, the farmers dug shallow wells for private use and deep wells for irrigation purposes because they found out that underground water was abundant.

Water from such wells or handy streams was, and in some places still is, drawn up with the aid of ancient devices. One such is the *dalu*, a bag that's raised and lowered by pulleys and ropes, which are pulled by a cow or camel walking up an inclined ramp. The other is the *shadoof*, which consists of a long wooden pole pivoted as a lever on a vertical post. A heavy stone, fixed to the short end of the lever, serves as a counterpoise to a bucket suspended by a rope from the long arm of the pole. In her drive to enter the twenty-first century, Libya is moving to mine her ground-water reserves. Scientists are concerned because this is stored water, and the scanty rainfall cannot be counted on to recharge the aquifers. If this water is mined, the water table will be drawn down so low that pumping will become costly and well yields will diminish.

Historically, therefore, we find that people in the East and the West have never stopped searching for potable water and, when necessary, devising ingenious methods of getting at it and transporting it. But before great supplies of water could be found and developed to serve our modern cities, industries, and farms, twentieth-century power drills and pumps first had to be invented. In addition, an understanding of hydrology had to be developed so that, with modern technology, the hidden sources of water could be efficiently located and economically explored and utilized.

What is hydrology?

Hydrology is the science of water—its behavior in the atmosphere, on the surface of the ground, and under the ground. Let's look into this science. We will find that water, which we very much take for granted, has some unique ways of its own.

3

The Hydrologic Cycle and the Fresh-Water Supply

Water is a replenishing resource. As vapor, it rises from land and sea to form rain clouds. As rain, it falls on mountains and meadows, cities and oceans. It waters the plants, saturates the soil, and percolates down to the water table. It flows into the rivers that flow into the sea. This is the water cycle—nature's "water wheel." Scientists call it the *hydrologic cycle.* It has no beginning and no end and is so simple in principle that it can be described in three words: evaporation, condensation, and precipitation.

Every year, some 95,000 cubic miles (395,998 cubic kilometers) of water evaporate from the surface of this planet. (A cubic mile is equivalent to an area twenty city blocks long, twenty wide, and twenty high.) Of this volume:

• 15,000 cubic miles (62,700 cubic kilometers) evaporate in part from the land—its lakes, ponds, streams, and other surfaces—and in part from the leaves of all living plants in a process called transpiration; and

• 80,000 cubic miles of water (333,472 cubic kilometers) evaporate from the ocean. Now, 80,000 cubic
miles of water removed from the ocean should, according
to mathematical computation, lower the surface by 39
inches (1 meter), but it doesn't because the vapor doesn't
remain in the atmosphere. Sooner or later it precipitates
in the form of liquid water drops or frozen crystals. Ultimately, through surface runoff, underground seepage,
evaporation, and other processes, all the water that is
brought to the land is returned to the ocean. Sometimes,
however, the return is delayed. Some of the water gets
frozen into glaciers for perhaps thousands of years; some
percolates deep into the ground and may remain there for
equally long periods.

Every drop of fresh water on this planet moves
through the hydrologic cycle endlessly. But don't be
fooled by its apparent constancy because it varies greatly
from time to time and place to place. In summer, for example, twice as much water evaporates as in winter. And

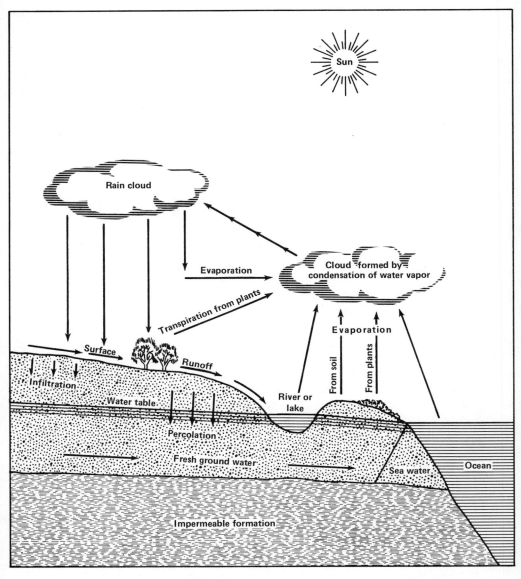

Diagram of the hydrologic cycle. (Gibson and Singer, Water Well Manual, *P.O. Box 4428, Berkeley, CA 94704)*

there are many dry places, deserts and glaciers, that receive only 1 inch (2.5 centimeters) of rain a year. On the other hand, there are many wet places, marshes and rain

Stalactites and stalagmites in Carlsbad Caverns, New Mexico. (USDI, National Park Service photo by George Grant)

forests, that may receive as much as 1, 2, or even 3 inches (2.5, 5.1, or 7.6 centimeters) of rain a day.

Still, the system as a whole is in wonderful balance. For every drop of water that evaporates skyward, a drop falls downward. Thus, the world's fresh-water supply remains fixed because it's locked into the cycle.

And yet the world's fresh-water supply is by no means always available to us as fresh and simon-pure. Sometimes it is, and then it's life-supporting; sometimes it isn't, and then it may be death-dealing; and in-between times it is often just so-so. Only as vapor is water pure— free of gases and minerals (chemical salts). As soon, however, as this vapor changes to rain, snow, or sleet, it begins to absorb some of the gases and minerals that are contained in the air. Consequently, when that rain, snow, or sleet falls to the ground, it is already contaminated.

Chief among those contaminants are:

• carbon dioxide and sulfur dioxide, which pour from the smokestacks of coal- and oil-fired furnaces; and

• nitrogen oxides, which spew from the tailpipes of cars and trucks, as well as from exploding volcanoes.

When carbon dioxide (CO_2) combines with water (H_2O), carbonic acid (H_2CO_3) is formed. When water is charged with carbonic acid, it becomes a solvent so strong that it leaches minerals out of the planet's boulders, ledges, rocks, and pebbles. It even hollows out huge caverns under rolling hills of limestone. Crisscrossed with labyrinths and often crowded with stalactites and stalagmites, some of them even have little streams flowing through them. Among the best known are the Carlsbad Caverns in New Mexico and the Postojna Grotto in Switzerland.

But when sulphur dioxide and the nitrogen oxides in the air combine with atmospheric water, then we really have trouble. Acid rain is formed, but it is not a new phenomenon. It forms whenever and wherever volcanoes erupt. However, since the 1950s, so much acid rain has fallen on some lakes in the Adirondacks, eastern Canada, and Scandinavia that the pH level (which expresses relative acidity or alkalinity) of the waters there dropped from a neutral 6 or 7 to 4 or 5, which is not far from pH 3, the reading for vinegar and lemon juice. Small wonder

The pH scale. (Acid Rain   EPA-600/9-79-036, July 1980, graphics by W. Welles)

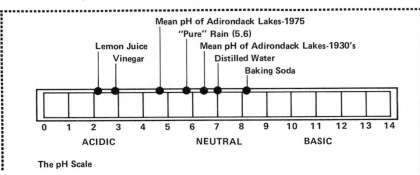

The pH Scale

that fish, frogs, and salamanders have disappeared from those waters. No longer do fishermen in glistening black hip boots wade into those lakes, which are now clear, blue, highly acidic, and dead.

If need be, we can live with poisoned, fishless lakes (horrid though that thought is), but can we live with rain that may contain acid as well as additional windblown contaminants: dust and dissolved minerals such as sodium, potassium, chloride, calcium, magnesium, bicarbonate, ammonia, and nitrate? Rain, you will remember, percolates into the ground and enters the ground-water supply. Of course, environmental scientists frequently

Liming an acidic pond in the Adirondack Mountains. (New York State Department of Environmental Conservation, photo by J. Georg)

test the pH of the lakes and apply lime to alkalize the water whenever necessary. But what about the rest of the earth's surface this kind of rain falls on?

Even in areas where private wells and public drinking-water supplies receive rain with a neutral pH that is judged to be safe, the water quality varies widely. In some instances, a high level of calcium and magnesium makes the water so "hard" that it won't behave the way it's expected to. Then county agents are deluged with complaints about shampoos and laundry soaps that don't make suds no matter how much is used, and about coffee that tastes bad. Where the water is really mineralized, as in some parts of Colorado near the geothermal springs, beauticians complain about hair-coloring problems—their blondes are turning green.

In rivers and lakes, an overabundance of dissolved minerals can make the water hazardous to marine life. In other instances, industrial plants that tap such watercourses find their pumps and pipelines damaged.

According to reports from USGS, rains have been known to dump more than 10,000 tons of calcium into the streams of southern Virginia and eastern North Carolina in a single month. More than 115,000 tons (104,328 metric tons) of dissolved minerals flow over Niagara Falls each and every day—an amount that computes to 80 tons (72.6 metric tons) a minute—enough to fill 80 one-ton trucks in that same minute.

Understandably, water isn't always exactly the same from place to place and from time to time. Its quality is changed as its chemical and physical composition is changed—in the air above and the ground below. In addition to the contaminants mentioned, there are also other salts, pesticides, and herbicides, as well as sewage and seepage from toxic dumps, constantly draining into the aquifers and waterways. And let's not forget the sediments—the sand, silt, clay, and gravel that wash down from the surrounding countryside.

It's because of these minerals and sediments that waterways are often named for the color of the load they carry. Who hasn't heard of the Red River of the North, which, draining through iron-rich lands, runs rusty red? And the Hwangho, popularly called the Yellow River because, flowing as it does through the loess plateaus of northern China, it picks up the yellow silty sediments? There are also Black Creeks, Brown Ponds, and Green Lakes, so named because they contain large amounts of dark organic matter: leaves, roots, plant remains, and algae.

Many of the pollutants we've been talking about are nature's own. Indeed, long before man began tossing his refuse around, nature was on the job as the original polluter, with her salts and sediments and organic matter. In this respect, nature never stops. The process is *ora e sempre*, from the Latin meaning now and forever.

So despite all the fresh water that's locked in the hydrologic cycle and despite the fact that only in recent times has man become a major polluter, access to potable water has been a problem since ancient times. Inscriptions from about 1450 B.C. on the walls of Egyptian tombs show a filtering apparatus in Thebes, on the Nile. This was designed to clarify such liquids as wine and water by letting them stand in huge jars until the sediments settled to the bottom. Then the clear liquids were siphoned off and enjoyed. Sanskrit records dating back three thousand years advise the people to keep their water in copper kettles, expose it to sunlight, and filter it through charcoal. Later, the Greeks and Romans constructed three-part settling cisterns, in which the water was held in sequence. This method seems to have worked well because, although they started with muddy river water, by the time it was drawn from the third compartment, it was clear enough to drink.

It was ever thus. Although the world's supply of fresh water kept circulating through the hydrologic cycle, it kept getting fouled up in the process. Eventually, however, that foul water reached the ocean. There it was recycled—distilled, if you will—and, as pure vapor, was again drawn skyward by the sun.

Throughout the millenniums, an understanding of the hydrologic cycle was pieced together with bits of superstition, homemade wisdom, magical lore, and science: first by ancient farmers, herders, well-diggers, and canal-builders—all practical men; then by philosophers who, sitting under village trees or in smoky taverns, argued endlessly about hypotheses and theories; and, more recently, by scientists searching for the essentials, the basics, the principles of hydrology. Always the spur to this piecing-together was need—the need, in the interests of survival, to understand three problems that wouldn't go away: the problems of water supply, water quality, and water management.

Since hydrology concerns the occurrence and behavior of water as well as its physical and chemical properties and its interaction with the environment, it's not surprising that this story should begin with the measurement of water. It started in rain-rich India, where the amount of rain that fell during a given season became a subject of considerable speculation in the fourth century B.C. In the interests of taxation, the lords and masters reasoned that, because there was a correlation between rainfall and the growth of the rice plants, the sensible thing to do was to measure the rain and tax the farmers accordingly.

Today, we know that measurement is the key to science and technology. Measurement provides the mathematical accuracy by which means comparisons can be made, conclusions drawn, and concepts verified. Except for those early practical rain gauges, which measured the rain that fell on the farm fields, scientific intelligence was only a matter of speculation for almost two thousand years.

With their logical and mathematical minds, the ancient Greek philosophers were the masters of speculation. Instead of attributing to the capricious gods the unpredictable behavior of water, the Greeks looked for what seemed to be *cause and effect*. The great Aristotle (who had been one of Plato's students and who himself had many students following him about wherever he walked and lectured) was one of those Greeks. He questioned, he philosophized, he argued, and he didn't hesitate to refer to the thinking of earlier philosophers. At last he came to a conclusion as novel as it was inaccurate: that rain was of minor significance to the world's fresh-water supply, as anyone who lived in Greece could see, because what rain there was barely wet the ground. Not being a world traveler, he didn't realize that Greece is a semiarid region that naturally receives little rainfall. He then theorized that streams, even the mightiest of them, originated in vast underground caverns where it was so cold that the air there condensed and released its water.

Other Greeks, as well as some of the later Romans, also subscribed to the cavern hypothesis and were quite convinced that rivers flowed from holes in the ocean bottom, through subsurface channels, to those caverns. From there, they said, the seawater was forced up into the mountains, where it dropped its salts and sediments and so became fresh and pure. The journey ended when the water broke through the earth's crust in the form of springs and rivers.

Actually, what we see here are philosophers trying to formulate a theory that, without taking atmospheric water into account, would explain the movement of water between land and sea. Even so, they had the water circulating the wrong way, from ocean *to* land. Later scientists, using scientific methods of observation and measurement, would discover that the water moved from land to ocean. But for long centuries, these explanations were accepted as gospel and supported as such by church and state. To think otherwise was heresy.

Bernard Palissy (1509–1589) was such a heretic. A French Huguenot and an acute observer, he made a point of saying that he was just an ordinary man, neither philosopher nor writer. Actually, he was a bit of a rebel and nearly lost his head after he joined a new religious movement called the Reformation and began talking about the origin of rivers and springs. What Palissy suggested was not only unheard of, it was downright unorthodox, contrary to accepted dogma. He maintained that the source of water for rivers and springs was *rain*.

It was the rain, the falling rain, that fed the springs and rivers, he told anyone who would listen. Not content with voicing these unconventional beliefs, he went so far as to write them down in a book, which he published in 1580, and what a furor that book created!

Palissy had had plenty of opportunities to observe the behavior of water. As a surveyor, he had trudged over hundreds of miles of countryside. He had clearly seen springs bubbling out of the ground in pastures and meadows, and he had seen brooks, creeks, and streams draining the gently rolling watersheds. Hadn't these watercourses run fuller and faster after every prolonged rainstorm? In addition, he was a geologist with some knowledge of underground rocks and rock formations—some bone dry, others dripping with moisture. Nevertheless, his opinions were heretical. He was thrown into jail, and his head was on the block.

It seems inconceivable now that at a time when Columbus had already discovered America, Cortez had conquered Mexico, and Magellan had sailed around the world, people should be beheaded or burned at the stake for opinions that stemmed from observation rather than from philosophical chitchat. Still, Palissy was lucky because he was also the ceramist who had invented enameled pottery. It was this latter accomplishment that saved his life. The Queen Mother, Catherine de Médicis, had been so pleased with his little enameled boxes that she promptly made him a member of the king's household and so immune to prosecution.

Book or no book, scientific contribution or not, Palissy received little recognition from the professional community. The old idea that seawater started from the ocean and flowed inland was entrenched and was to remain so for another ninety years.

Not until the end of the seventeenth century were the ideas of Palissy to be considered, reconsidered, reexamined, and put to the test—this time by another Frenchman, Pierre Perrault. A lawyer by profession, Perrault (1608–1680) was more interested in amateur science and natural philosophy than in donning wig and robe and picking up the legal cudgels to try cases in court. Perrault was the first to measure hydraulic components seriously. Knowing that every bucketful of water that falls from the clouds must go someplace, he reasoned that if he could measure those bucketfuls and figure out what happens to all that water, he'd have some scientific answers.

Accordingly Perrault set off to arrange for testing this hypothesis in the upper Seine River watershed. Using the best rain gauges he could get, he began working on a three-year project that was to turn people's thinking around. He measured the rainfall in that region and found that it averaged 19.11 inches (48.54 centimeters) a year. He figured out that one-sixth of the total volume of that fallen rain was carried off by the Seine River, out to the English Channel. Of the other five-sixths, he estimated that some drained into the ground, some evaporated, and some, after being absorbed by plants, transpired from the leaves into the atmosphere.

These findings Perrault published in 1674. His conclusions couldn't have been stated more clearly. "Rain and snow water," he wrote, "were adequate—not only to sustain stream flow but also to make fountains [springs] and rivers run perpetually."

In the field of science, it is customary for one man's findings to be challenged, checked, and verified by another and yet another before they are accepted. With the intellectual climate beginning to change at that time, it wasn't long before Perrault's conclusions concerning precipitation measurements were confirmed without any political hassles. The confirmer was a scientifically minded religious, Edme Mariotte, prior of the Monastery of Saint Martin-sous-Neaune. However, although both Perrault and Mariotte had measured the amount of water that fell from the atmosphere and accounted for its disposition after it reached the ground, although both noted that one-sixth was returned to the sea, neither explained what happened to that one-sixth after it mingled with sea-water. Did it remain in the ocean? If it did, why hadn't the surface of the oceans risen and risen and drowned the continents? Surely that one-sixth had to be returned to the atmosphere because without such a return, without such replenishment, the atmosphere would soon become drier than dry.

Clearly the hydrologic cycle is composed of three arcs through which the earth's fresh water moves: along the surface, under the ground, and in the atmosphere. It now remained for the English astronomer Edmund Halley (1656–1742) to close the atmospheric arc of the cycle.

Learned, outgoing, jovial, and a great eater, Halley was an amazing many-sided genius. He was as fascinated by the starry heavens as by the ocean depths, and liked nothing better than to go exploring the ocean bottom in a cumbersome old diving bell. Since the bell was neither comfortable nor efficient, he invented a diving suit! In fact, he invented so many things in line with his count-less interests that every morning at the breakfast table, his wife accused him of throwing away the family fortune on useless scientific experiments.

It was one of those experiments that enabled Halley to conclude that the amount of water evaporated from the ocean was exactly enough to produce the rain that re-plenished the rivers that flowed into the ocean. Of course, such an astonishing conclusion was loudly rejected by the diehards, but it hasn't ever been disproved. This conclu-sion stemmed from a simple little experiment Halley car-ried out with an 8-inch (20.32-centimeter) pan of salt water, a beam scale, a thermometer, and a bucket of burning coals. He filled the pan with 4 inches (10 centimeters) of a 3.5-percent salt solution (which is equivalent to ocean salinity) and set it on the scale over the coals, heating the water to the temperature of a hot summer day. He kept that temperature steady, and he recorded the diminishing weight of the pan as more and more water evaporated from it. After two hours, of watching and recording and countless hours of mathematical computation, Halley was able to extrapolate, or estimate, the amount of evaporation that annually takes place over the Mediterranean Sea and to conclude that the volume of water so *lost* from the Mediterranean equaled the volume of water that the inflowing rivers *returned* to it. Later, he was able to compute the amount of water vapor that escaped from the ocean and again was able to show that the ocean was replenished by an equal amount of river water. That's how Halley closed the atmospheric arc of the hydrologic cycle!

With the cycle conceptualized, the science of hydrology was founded. In time, this science, enriched with new understandings, would enable man to use the world's fresh-water supply more efficiently. Simultaneously, however, a couple of problems surfaced:
  • scientific problems of hydrology began to challenge the new scientists; and
  • economic, social, and political problems of water supply and management began to challenge the people.

4

The Industrial Revolution and the Water Sciences

Time . . . the eighteenth century.

Place . . . England.

As soon as the science of hydrology was founded, it, together with other emerging sciences, immediately intermeshed with a new-style revolution. This was a revolution in socio-political thinking, and it challenged the belief that it's enough for science to tell the truth about the world—no more and no less.

That belief has long since been discredited. Thanks to the work of those two redoubtable scholars John Locke and Adam Smith, it's now commonly accepted that scientific inquiry is a social undertaking geared to social responsibility. In a word, science has a job to do for the betterment of man, although it doesn't always work out that way.

The seventeenth-century English philosopher Locke (1632–1704) had expounded the rights of the individual. Later, the Scottish economist Smith (1723–1790) preached the doctrine of laissez faire (the theory that government should intervene as little as possible in economic affairs). At the same time, in the colonies across the Atlantic, corsetmaker Thomas Paine (1737–1809) picked up his quill pen and became a fiery political writer. Paine's publications *Common Sense* and *The Rights of Man* raised the concept of individualism to a national concern. The upshot of all this teaching and preaching and political rhetoric was the emergence of a brand-new concept: that every man is responsible for his own salvation, socially and politically. This was such an inflammatory concept that, spreading as it did among traders and miners, craftsmen, laborers, and peasants, it would topple governments in the not too distant future. This concept also forged the industrial revolution, which was propelled by water.

To self-taught engineers and eager entrepreneurs, water was the element for building a canal system, not for pleasure craft, but for barges that would bring to the country villages what the country people needed to keep their home industries going: tons of coal and iron, bales of wool and cotton, iron nails, tools, and more.

Of special help to the canal-builders were the hydrologists, who mapped the surface waters, studied their volume, their rate of evaporation, and their recharge by rain. They also studied stream gauging and river discharge. With this added knowledge, they were able to help venturesome businessmen plan for the construction of dams and reservoirs, as well as water wheels for gristmills and sawmills. Naturally, business flourished then. Home industries expanded, and just as naturally, blacksmiths and carpenters, weavers and millers and ceramists grew quite prosperous.

Because the canals promoted commercial navigation on such a grand scale, a new kind of boat—a boat that was highly durable and manageable—was needed to ply those waters and carry heavy cargo. No problem. This was the beginning of the age of science and invention, so in due time there it was, an iron boat built according to newly understood scientific and technological principles. Ironmaster John Wilkinson (1728–1808), using cast iron, built that boat—the first of its kind in the world—and he sailed it under an iron bridge. What a marvelous accomplishment! Wilkinson was so carried away by cast iron and what could be done with it that he had himself buried in an iron coffin at the time of his death.

Who could ever describe the pseudoscientific excitement of those days? Scientists and engineers, the rich, the poor, and the unschooled hastened to appropriate a shack, a woodshed, a closet, or a corner in a basement and started inventing. There were hundreds of inventions, all designed to do the work of human hands. Of those, three in particular helped to revolutionize the manufacture of cotton cloth and so got the industrial era underway: the carding machine and the spinning jenny, which were invented by James Hargreaves, an illiterate weaver; and the new, improved steam engine, which was created by James Watt, a Scottish maker of mathematical instruments and a mechanical genius.

Suddenly, water wasn't just water any more—for

drinking, bathing, watering crops, or turning mill wheels. With Watt's improved steam engine, water, as exploding steam, was power—power on a previously undreamed-of scale. As steam, water now drove the carding and spinning machines in the newly built factories and produced textiles so cheaply and so quickly that it all seemed like beautiful magic. This is how it worked. Wood or coal-fired furnaces heated boilers full of water. The water got hotter and hotter until it turned to steam. The steam was led off to the engine, and then—with a hum, a roar, and an unstoppable clatter—the textile mills rolled. Almost immediately, villages grew into towns, and as the furnaces multiplied and chimney stacks reached higher, black smoke darkened the countryside and proclaimed industrial prosperity.

To the factory workers, however—to the men, women, and thousands of children ages seven and up who lived in crowded, unsanitary hovels flanking the mills—all this industrial activity was not beautiful magic. It was diabolical magic, something the devil himself might have thought up. Speed was the credo of the day. Time was money. Even the Sunday schools doubled their efforts to teach the children that sloth—slowness and idleness—was sinful. It was not to be countenanced because "Satan finds some mischief still/For idle hands to do." But as the machines made the factories ever more efficient, some workers had to be discharged. As unemployment increased, so did vandalism. Clandestine groups known as Machine Wreckers would break into the factories and demolish the machines.

However, once the new scientific technology was understood by the men of business, once the profits began rolling in with dizzying speed, there was no turning back to the old slow ways of handwork. The factories were rebuilt and enlarged. Prosperity skyrocketed. And the newly rich built homes resembling castles and mansions, which they set in the middle of wide meadows that soon turned into sweeping, velvety lawns. And water was everywhere—in gushing fountains, rippling duck ponds, tree-bordered reflecting pools, and meandering streams afloat with tiny skiffs.

How was it then that water, science, and technology, which had so gloriously powered the English industrial revolution, bypassed the poor and left them stranded in their unwholesome surroundings?

The answer lies in the fact that at the same time water can be power, it can also be a scourge. Some of the medical men of those days—the apothecaries, midwives,

A water carrier in old London. (*From Smiles,* Lives of Engineers, *1862*)

and barbers, whose spinning red-and-white barber poles advertised the fact that they did a bit of doctoring on the side—vaguely suspected that water, which can heal, can also kill. They saw what the cultured and well-to-do never saw. They saw working people packed into makeshift quarters in the factory towns. They saw these people dipping water from filthy streams, scooping it out of dirty, unprotected springs, and buying it from open buckets lugged about by water peddlers. And they saw these people—whole families at a time—dying like flies from what we now know are waterborne diseases: cholera, typhoid, and infectious hepatitis. They saw the surface waters polluted by man-made and factory-made wastes. Surmising that there might be a connection between water and disease, they prescribed well water as medicine for those who could afford to pay for it.

Although well water, drawn from under the ground, is generally of good quality, it didn't—and still doesn't—always rate A for health and safety. Even as the polluted river, pond, or other surface water plagued the English in their sooty towns, persistent floods of acidic black water often plagued the men in the coal mines. For dewatering those mines and keeping them dewatered, hydraulic engineers needed powerful pumps. These they would have, but not for decades, not until after the 1850s, when the Bessemer process and the open-hearth process of steelmaking had been developed. Necessity is indeed the mother of invention, but the miners were an endangered species as long as they lacked powerful pumps to make the mines safe and dry to work in. So powerful pumps were invented right after steel became available.

For the city's poor, who were afflicted by waterborne diseases, science could not then provide a cure. Few medical men were perceptive enough and astute enough to document, from personal observation, the connection between foul water and cholera, which periodically and violently swept England and much of the world. Only Dr. John Snow, of London, supported by Dr. William Budd, of Bristol, had come to the conclusion that something in the water the cholera victims drank was responsible for the onset of the disease. Because these gentlemen had no scientific proof with which to back their conclusions, they were attacked and ridiculed by the medical establishment. Conservative men of medicine could no more accept the idea that water could be a carrier of disease than they could envision the highly engineered waterworks that would be filtering and treating raw water so as to provide a safe product to industrialized towns in the next century.

These then were some of the dazzling benefits and some of the deadly and debilitating problems of water that were part and parcel of the industrial revolution in England. As other countries also became industrialized, they, too, faced similar pluses and minuses. Wherever machines hummed and black smoke billowed from chimney stacks, there, too, prosperity became the order of the day. And as the population grew denser in the factory towns, so too did the surface and underground waters become dangerously polluted. All industrialized countries needed to find ways of treating surface waters so they were fit to drink and ways of exploring underground sources for additional potable supplies.

Looking back, it's easy to say that what that industrial era needed was a good water-management program of discovery, treatment, transport, and distribution. For more than a century now, hydrologists and other water experts have given the study of, and the search for, ground water the highest priority, but though we are near the end of the twentieth century, do we, even in the industrialized world, have all the good water management programs we need?

In the main, we do not. We have only to look at a newspaper to be reminded of our water problems.

Do we know how to solve them?

Of course we do.

What's holding us back?

The public will is weak because it's uninformed. Although the public is familiar with surface water, it is not equally familiar with ground water, which is thirty-five times more abundant.

5

Searching for Water Under the Ground

In the search for water, old-timers often tapped the underground. Hadn't they successfully tunneled thousands of miles of horizontal wells in western Asia and northeast Africa? Hadn't they excavated such deep "grandfather wells" in the Holy Land and China that it took all of three generations to complete just one of them? And, more recently, hadn't most farmers, except those living alongside rivers and lakes, dug their own wells on their own land so they'd have enough drinking water for themselves and their animals? Still, for a farmer to dig a well was a chancy thing unless he was luckily located and could read the clues that nature scattered about.

One clue had to do with the water table. In some lowland regions, the water table was sometimes so high that it actually emerged above ground. Then the water swamped the meadows, bubbled out in springs, or collected in lakes and ponds. Other times it ran off in rills and brooks, creeks and streams. In such places, who could doubt that water was underfoot? A shovel, a pickax, a crowbar, and a pair of strong swinging arms, and there, in a few hours or a day at most, was a well brimming with water.

The scenario was different in desert regions. There the sun was blistering hot, the sand glittering, the rain scarce, and the water table very low in all but a few spots. So desert dwellers needed to look for other clues. They looked for wild and growing plants and they found two kinds:

• the drought-resistant xerophytes (pronounced zir-a-fites), most of which belong to the cactus family and store what little water they can get inside their leaves and stems; and

• the water-loving phreatophytes (pronounced free-at-a-fites), which include mesquite, salt grass, and grease-wood. These plants take up residence, so to speak, where their long roots can reach the deep-seated water table. In such semiarid areas as the American Southwest, cotton-wood and willow trees broadcast, "Water below." That's why desert settlements often cluster around thickets of such plants.

These are good clues, and the men and women who grew up on the land learned to see what the land showed them. Still, the siting of a well in those particular places was as often as not awkward: too far from the house or barn, too near for sanitary reasons, or altogether too stony for even the stoutest pickax. However, trying to pinpoint a likely spot closer to the house was a gamble. A dug hole, even a deep one, didn't always produce a reliable, year-round well, although the nearest neighbor, a short mile away, might have more water than he could use splashing out of a shallow spring. Small wonder that locating water under the ground seemed touched with mysticism.

In the absence of scientific understanding, mystical explanations were as good as any, and so it came to pass that water witches, diviners, and dowsers—all one and the same—came to be held in high esteem. Could they not, with a forked branch or a so-called divining rod, stroll across a field and locate hidden deposits of water? Often enough, they seemed to do just that.

Divining, or dowsing as it is generally called, has a long history. According to the American Society of Dowsers, it started at least eight thousand years ago. A large, carbon-dated drawing on the side of a cave in the Atlas Mountains of North Africa shows a dowser in action, surrounded by onlookers. Later, the Chinese practiced dowsing, as Marco Polo found when he traveled there. And by the time that Columbus returned from the New World, the divining rod was in common use throughout Europe. This practice, however, so aroused the wrath of that religious rebel Martin Luther (1483–1564) that he told his followers in no uncertain terms that searching for water this way was tampering with the Unseen in the Underground. Other clerics following his lead, nailed injunctions to their church doors and also forbade the practice. Still, equally devout religious people must have thought otherwise because in 1568 a fresh-water source was located for St. Theresa in Spain with, it is claimed, the aid of dowsers.

This practice continued to spread to the far corners of the world—wherever the Europeans explored and colonized—because the new settlers needed water in a hurry and believed that the dowsers could find it for them every time. Even today, in the 1980s, there are some 25,000 dowsers with their forked branches and brass rods operating in rural America, searching for veins of water for property owners wanting a well.

Geologists take exception to the idea of dowsers promising to find veins of water. For one thing, they say, anybody can promise he'll find water under the ground and he might—not because his branch jerks downward at a given spot, but because there's water underfoot almost everywhere—if you drill deep enough. But *veins of water!* There's no such thing, although it is true there are small streams underground. These streams flow in *solution channels*, in crevices, that were enlarged and extended by percolating water charged with that powerful solvent carbonic acid. (See the photograph on page 62.)

There are all kinds of crevices and openings in the subsurface rocks. There are cracks and joints called *fractures*, and there are *seams* between the layered formations. Even when these fractures and seams are hairline thin, water seeps into them.

Ground water is not a simple subject, but geologists and their coprofessionals, the hydrologists, are eager to explain what it is and how it ties in with the rocks below, the atmosphere above, and the streams that flow into the sea. They're ready to walk you off your feet on a field trip to trace the source of water that's dripping out of rocks at a roadside cut; ready to ride you in a Land Rover over nonexistent roads to explore water-bearing rock layers slanting into riverbanks, gorges, chasms, and canyons; ready to fly you in a survey plane to photograph the lay of the land below.

A small stream flowing through a solution channel in Mammoth Cave, Kentucky, is large enough for small-boat riding. (USDI, National Park Service)

How do you find such obliging fellows? You write to the United States Department of the Interior (or its counterpart in other countries) and ask where the nearest USGS office is located. Then, if you have a serious and enthusiastic interest in rocks and the water they hold, you visit that USGS office. You ask intelligent questions and you scrape up an acquaintance with a friendly and amenable scientist.

This author met such a ground-water scientist when she called at a USGS office in the Tri-State area.

"Look," he said, "ground rules first. You may quote me, but not by name or address because, in this office we aren't equipped to receive all your readers who might want to spend the day with us or go trailing after us on a field trip."

"Okay. Ground rules accepted."

Mr. X, an energetic fellow, began to bustle around the organized clutter in his office as he reached for the things he was talking about: illustrated ground-water reports stuffed in desk drawers, aerial photographs heaped on tables, and map rolls stuck into umbrella-like racks. He told me that when he goes to the field, he crams his pockets with the geological paraphernalia he's likely to need on that particular investigation, starting with a pocket stereoscope for checking elevations and depressions on his aerial maps, a compass for checking the marks on bedrock, a hand lens for noting rock crystals and hairline cracks, and a bottle of dilute acid for verifying the rock chemistry. Maps, jars for sediments, sample bags for rocks, and a pointy hammer go into his knapsack. If he's off to pump samples—to collect water from wells, rivers, lakes, or ponds for chemical analysis—he makes sure to stow some gallon jugs and a small pump (of the hand, gasoline, or electric variety) into the USGS station wagon, which is already equipped with filters and a small refrigerator. If he's off to a promising well site for which no information is available, he arranges for test drillings.

"So now you want to know about ground water," he said. "Well, ground water is part of the land drainage system, and it all starts with precipitation—with the rain and snowmelt that does *not* enter the streams."

Mr. X took a turn around his office and decided to explain further. "When we talk about ground water, we talk about that portion of the rain and snowmelt that actually seeps into the ground. There, some of it is retained as soil moisture, while the balance seeps to the water table, where it becomes ground water. It's the ground water that moves through the soil and rocks below until it *ultimately* discharges into the stream beds or the tidewater."

"So is that the reason that most streams rarely dry up even during prolonged drought?" I asked.

"Exactly," he said. "It's a wonderful system."

63

Ground, or subsurface, water represents about two-thirds of the world's fresh-water reserves. But note: the world's fresh-water reserves represent less than 1 percent of all the water on this planet. It is within 1 mile (1.6 kilometers) of the earth's surface—1 mile underfoot—that ground water is stored. Half of it lies within the lower half-mile and is beyond the reach of conventional drilling tools. The rest of it moves through the aquifers in the upper half mile and serves as the source for well water.

Aquifers vary so much in location and size that they've given more than one hydrologist a lifelong headache. Aquifers may lie near the surface or at great depth. They may be hundreds of miles in length and breadth, or they may be so narrow and shallow—almost like ribbons running through rock—that of two adjoining farms, only one owner may have a good supply of water. Additionally, aquifers may run every which way. They may be horizontal or vertical, slanty or even bowl-shaped. No matter how they run, they invariably fall into one of two categories.

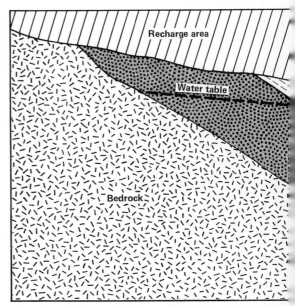

Diagram of a confined or artesian aquifer and recharge area. The potentiometric surface is the imaginary level to which water will rise in tightly cased wells. (U.S. Geological Survey)

The first is the *unconfined* aquifer, which is more or less close to the surface. It is topped by a mass of unconsolidated materials, such as sand, gravel, and mixed-up glacial till. This kind of aquifer rests on an impervious—that is, non-porous—bed of rock or clay. A well drilled into an unconfined aquifer usually provides enough water for the average household. In many instances, it may serve large public waterworks.

"But the category 2 aquifer—the *confined* aquifer—is something else," said Mr. X. "It may be found at almost any level, and no matter which way it runs, it's invariably sandwiched between layers of impervious material. Here the water is contained under hydrostatic or confined pressure, as if it were in an enormous main. It doesn't ripple and run and slosh; neither does it just sit there, immobilized. It is propelled by pressure and gravity, and so it has to keep moving from one rock fracture or seam to another and to yet another. Note this unique feature of a confined aquifer: its water will rise above the aquifer's level when tapped by a

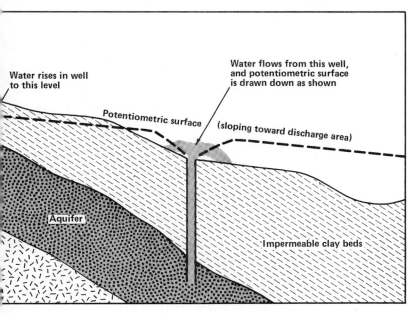

Water rises in well to this level

Water flows from this well, and potentiometric surface is drawn down as shown

Potentiometric surface

(sloping toward discharge area)

Aquifer

Impermeable clay beds

well. [See the diagram on pages 64-65.] This constant movement of ground water accounts for the changes in its quality, hydrostatic pressure, and temperature."

Mention has already been made of the fact that moving water leaches minerals out of rocks, and it is these minerals, together with seeped-in waste, that account for the differences found in water quality.

As for the hydrostatic pressure that exists in a confined aquifer, a well-driller who is unfamiliar with the underground geology might be in for a surprise because as soon as his drill bit penetrates the aquifer, the water rises or even spurts up like a fountain and continues to flow for who knows how long. This is called an *artesian well*, named after those legendary free-flowing French wells in the province of Artois. Ground water may have to travel to such wells from enormous distances. That's why artesian wells in Kansas, located at the base of a bowl-shaped aquifer, may be spurting water from the Rocky Mountains on the west and from the Appalachian Mountains on the east. As for temperature changes, these occur as an aquifer dips deeper into the earth because heat increases with depth as much as 50 to 100 degrees F per mile (10 to 37 degrees C per 1.6 kilometer). Additionally, if the aquifer happens to come in contact with magma, hot dry rock, or a radioactive deposit, then the cold water that enters the aquifer really heats up and might return to the surface as hot. A case in point is Warm Springs, in Georgia, where for years thousands of polio victims, including the late President Franklin Delano Roosevelt, have gone for relief. According to geologists, this warm spring water comes from the Hollis aquifer, which starts with cold rain at an intake area, not far from the village. At first, the Hollis runs northward for about a mile, at a depth of several hundred feet, where its temperature increases to 62 degrees F (16.6 degrees C). Then it plunges downward until it runs smack into a horizontal floor of impervious rock. Blocked, the water, which is now under considerable pressure, is forced upward along an alternate route and bubbles out in the springs at a temperature of 88 degrees F (31.1 degrees C).

The movement of water under artesian conditions is one thing, but computing the *rate* at which water flows through an aquifer is what makes the job of the groundwater explorer so difficult. An experienced hydrogeologist, Mr. X says that "under natural conditions, water moves through aquifers at rates ranging from a few feet per year to a few feet per day. So who can tell, for example, how long some of the water that's pumped out in Milwaukee, Wisconsin, has been traveling that short 25-mile (40-kilometer) stretch of aquifer that runs from Oconomowoc, where the rain and snowmelt first entered it?" Add to this two other inputs that have been traveling for indeterminate distances: the precipitated atmospheric water that fell over the length and breadth of the aquifer, and the underground seepage from lakes and stream beds, as well as from mines, landfills, toxic dumps, cesspools, and septic tanks. Then ask yourself how anyone, drawing a pail of water from his kitchen sink in Milwaukee, could compute the rate at which each of those water drops journeyed to get there.

The rate of movement in the aquifer is important to anyone about to have a well drilled on his property. Will the well deliver 50 gallons a minute, or 100, or a measly 2? (A gallon equals 3.8 liters.) So many factors are involved that it's hard to tell before the actual drilling because flow is affected not only by pressure and gravity but also by the size of the openings in the rocks. The situation aboveground must also be taken into consideration. If excessive precipitation sends water seeping into the aquifer faster than the aquifer can discharge it to springs, wells, lakes, streams, and distant seas, then the water table will rise so rapidly that some areas will become swamped and others actually flooded.

If you've ever lived on a farm and were in the habit of glancing into the open well every time you went to fetch a pail of water, you surely noticed the level of the water shining down there. That was the local water table. If you saw that the water table was falling and if you were wise, you began to think abut irrigating your garden. If you saw that the water table was rising, you began to prepare for a little flooding in your root cellar. All this you knew before the TV broadcasters told you so.

Such an acquaintance with the water table is commendable, but much more is needed when a public waterworks or a great irrigation project is to be constructed. Then a high-powered scientific team must be called in to map and evaluate the underground structure with the latest techniques. These include:

• *electrical resistivity*, which measures the resistance that underground rocks at a given depth offer to an electrical current; and

• *seismic reflection*, which measures the speed at which sound waves, caused by a surface explosion, travel through the ground for a given distance.

Such findings are invaluable to the water-seekers because they show whether the rocks there are porous or nonporous. Where the rocks are porous, you can expect to find an aquifer. Additionally, hydrologists study aerial photographs for such surface clues as drainage patterns, large outcrop areas of bedrock, and pits and hollows, as well as stands of forest and other vegetative coverings. Nor should we forget to mention that newest technological marvel, the electronic computer, which helps the scientists chart the movement of ground water. However, for a really complete picture of what's going on in that dark underground, the hydrogeologists need to study yet another factor: the *recharge rate* of a given aquifer.

As long as an aquifer's recharge by precipitation and seepage equals its natural discharge, the volume of water within the aquifer remains nearly constant. Under such conditions, both water companies and users are content, and the water supply is taken for granted. But let a community expand, let new power plants erect great cooling towers, let lush, verdant lawns become high priority with homeowners, and water problems are likely to develop. As pumpage increases, the aquifer's discharge rate may exceed its recharge rate. If this should occur, the water table will fall, and if it falls low enough, the water supply may dwindle to a critical point. What happens then? The wells go deeper and the pumping bills go higher. At the same time, water quality deteriorates and costly treatment becomes necessary. If the bills get to be too exorbitant, then wells with plenty of water still in them may be abandoned, and the community may be reduced to such a state of decline that families pack up and leave. Of course, such an eventuality would be bad for the people, but in this instance what's bad for the people is good for the aquifer. With the people gone, pumping would be reduced to zero. Then natural recharge would, in time, fill the aquifer, saturate it, and raise the water table to its original level. Once again there would be plenty of water trickling through.

By the 1980s, the water table had dropped alarmingly in many of the world's agricultural, industrial, and residential regions. Why? Because pumpage had exceeded the natural recharge rate of the aquifers. As a result, subsidence or sinking of the land has occurred in places. In some residential areas of Texas, so much ground water had been pumped out that salty water from nearby Galveston Bay intruded into the aquifers and emerged as unwanted ponds. (See the photograph on page 70.) In some parts of California's San Joaquin Valley, overpumpage caused the clay beds to compact. Then the land subsided to such an extent that the roofs of some houses and the tops of some telephone poles were on a level with the nearby lawns. Shortages caused by overpumping were also beginning to be reported in the American High Plains, where the Ogallala aquifer is sending out distress signals. The water table there is dropping 3 to 6 inches (7.6 to 15.2 centimeters) a year. Said to be one of the largest fresh-water aquifers in the world, the Ogallala covers 150,000 square miles (388,500 square kilometers)

A pond, formed by the intrusion of salt water from Galveston Bay, replaces a lawn in Baytown, Texas. (USDA, Soil Conservation Service photo by George C. Marks)

and contains 2 billion acre feet of water. (An acre foot is the amount of water that would cover one acre to a depth of one foot.) Its importance? It provides more water to farmers than the Colorado River and has been supplying water to irrigate the cotton fields of Texas and New Mexico, as well as the wheat and corn fields of Kansas, Colorado, Oklahoma, and southern Nebraska. In some areas, farmers, already aware that this water supply is dwindling, have started to replace wheat and corn acreage with less thirsty crops, such as cotton and sorghum. And lawmakers, apprised of the fact that the Ogallala may be overpumped and drained dry by the year 2000, have passed legislation granting water-depletion allowances to the grain growers.

In the United States, overpumpage has been increasing, exceeding the natural rate of recharge for a number of reasons. For one, the per-capita rate of consumption has risen to 190 gallons (718 liters). This is due in part to the wasteful practices of the average American. It is also due in part to the increased demand for water that comes with technology. High-rise buildings are often completely sealed and must, therefore, run on air conditioning year-round. There is an ever increasing number of computer centers that call for great quantities of water. Additionally, when city streets and roads are coated with asphalt or concrete, natural precipitation cannot seep into the ground. Instead, it runs off to the sewers and is lost.

Still, prospects are getting brighter. Although we have yet to learn how to use our water supply efficiently, some scientists are showing us one way out of the dilemma. Instead of waiting for natural recharge to fill depleted ground-water reservoirs or aquifers, they are advising artificial recharge.

Aquifers can be recharged artificially with *surplus* water injected into recharge wells. It may sound strange to talk of a surplus when communities are stricken by shortages, but indeed there is a surplus in the form of used water that's generally discharged from such facilities as air-conditioning plants and cooling towers and from highly polluted waste water that's drained from kitchens and bathrooms, swimming pools, slaughter houses, and the like.

Swedish engineers in Stockholm and Uppsala report that they have been recharging their aquifers with partially treated waste water. They call attention to the fact that this treated water, traveling through the ground reservoir, gets naturally filtered and purified in the process and so increases their potable supply. In other areas, such as southern California and the sand dunes of Holland, treated waste water has been pumped into recharge wells for another purpose: to build a water barrier against intruding seawater that was mineralizing the underground supply serving the local communities.

It should, however, be stressed that, in some instances, artificial recharge is virtually impossible, as you can see by what happened in New York City's borough of

Brooklyn. There, the Brooklyn Water Company pumped so much water out of the ground that the water table dropped markedly in the vicinity of the wells, causing the depressed water surface to assume the shape of an inverted cone, which scientists call a *cone of depression*. As pumping continued, this cone continued to deepen until its tip reached down 36 feet (11 meters) below sea level. Its rim circled an area 10 miles (16 kilometers) in diameter, and the whole district came to resemble a vast crater. When the rim finally edged the ocean, seawater began flowing inland, to the wells. The upshot? Since pumps can't tell the difference between seawater and fresh water, salt water began running out of the taps in kitchens and bathrooms. The wells were then shut down, the water company went out of business, and Brooklyn's water pipes had to be hooked into the New York City water supply, which is drawn from an upland source, 200 miles (322 kilometers) away.

Can't they clean out the Brooklyn aquifer? Yes they can, but only with great difficulty. At the rate water moves underground, such an undertaking would take many decades. It would also be prohibitively expensive.

We've been talking about surpluses that can be injected into recharge wells and in this way can give the aquifers and the people a second chance at the same old water. But there's yet another source of surplus water— that which falls from the sky during months of high precipitation.

Seasonal surpluses can be impounded in underground reservoirs by a system called *spreading*. With this system, excess water is withdrawn from swollen and overflowing ponds and streams and allowed to spread aboveground in selected basins, furrows, and ditches that are underlain by sand and gravel. There, the spread water percolates down to the aquifer, where it remains, in underground storage, until it is needed—in the hot, dry months of summer.

As the thirsty twentieth century draws to a close,

many hydrologists are beginning to look upon the artificial recharging of aquifers as a neat way to trap water from the hydrologic cycle in order to assure ourselves of an increased supply of ground water.

So much for the underground arc of the cycle. But what about the other two arcs: on the surface of the ground and in the air? If hydrologists can learn how to trap water in those two arcs, they'll be on their way to regulating the hydrologic cycle itself.

Can they do it? It's a challenge, a challenge that's intriguing and fascinating and of the highest importance to the well-being of man.

6

Searching for Usable Surface Water

Ancient man's search for usable surface water depended on his legs, his dreams, and the portents he received from nature. These methods served him right into the fifteenth and sixteenth centuries—into the Age of Discovery, when daring adventurers roamed the seas, hoping to find new lands. Even then, unless those sailing men were lucky enough to anchor at the mouth of a sweet-flowing stream, they had to set out on foot or on burro or on horseback to search for water that was drinkable or, in the case of Ponce de Leon, water that would restore youth.

The seventeenth and eighteenth centuries saw sailing ships taking colonists to those newly discovered lands. As with the explorers, the first concern was for a visible supply of usable water. When they found it, in ponds and lakes and rivers, that's where they settled. By the nineteenth century, however, various governments were launching dual-purpose exploratory expeditions. One purpose was academic—to add to the knowledge of the world.

The other was economic—to locate natural resources and make sure there was plenty of water nearby.

In the Americas, it was Thomas Jefferson, third President of the United States, whose interest in waterways such as the rampaging Ohio River triggered the great movement of continental exploration in 1803. No sooner had he authorized the Louisiana Purchase than he sent the Lewis and Clark Expedition through this new territory to Oregon and on to the Pacific. Off they went with their mules and their horses, their canoes and other small river craft. Off they went through uncharted river valleys and over great mountain ranges. Often they were treed by grizzly bears. More often they were chased by hostile Indians. Occasionally they were received by friendly Indians. When the expedition returned two years and four months later, they had traveled over 8,000 miles (12,874 kilometers) and had so thoroughly mapped the territory, so carefully recorded the overland routes and waterways, ponds, lakes, and watering holes, that within a generation the Oregon Trail had become a doorway to western trade. In 1869 another doorway to western trade was opened when the American geologist John Wesley Powell sailed down the hazardous Colorado River.

Similar expeditions were subsequently mounted for the same reasons in South America, in the "dark continent" of Africa, and in the ice-bound reaches of the Arctic and the Antarctic.

By the twentieth century, as world population increased, the search for surface waters accelerated. By mid-century, hydrogeologists were flying small survey planes and taking aerial photographs of small segments of the terrain. By taping consecutive photographs together, they were able to map a given area and so locate the visible water sources. In 1972, Landsat was hurled into the sky. Landsat is a satellite that scans the earth and reports on our total environment: the land, the water, and the air. It orbits the planet every eighteen days at an altitude of 575 miles (925 kilometers). It "images" a 115-square-mile (298-square-kilometer) area every twenty-five seconds and converts these images to photographs. Then the scientists who are concerned with water resources can locate and analyze the rivers and lakes and wetlands, the flooded areas, and the degree of pollution. Additionally, they can use this Landsat data not only for local areas but also for regional and global areas.

With such a complete photographic layout, anyone can see that there are lakes by the thousands, and rivers— some of them so extensive that they look like a drawing of bare-branched trees in winter. These surface waters may be naturally fresh and potable, or they may not. They may be naturally long-lived and endure for thousands of years, or they may not. (See the photograph on page 77.)

To understand the reasons for the variations in water quality and duration, it is necessary to understand some-

What might appear as a picture of a burning tree is actually an aerial view of the Colorado River Delta in Lower California. (U.S. Geological Survey)

thing of the life history of these bodies of water. Let's start with lakes.

Lakes (and ponds too, of course) are located in natural depressions into which the surrounding waters drain. These depressions may have been created by ice or fire. They may have been scooped out by continental ice sheets or creeping alpine glaciers that dumped rock deposits across a valley. They may have been formed by landslides that thundered *smack!* into a stream or by earthquakes. Russia's Lake Baikal, which is 1 mile (1.6 kilometers) deep, is one example. There are also so-called bottomless lakes, which are nothing more than water-filled volcanic craters, and other lakes that were formed by red-hot lava flowing across a riverbed and damming it.

Lakes may have an everlasting look about them, but their waters are never static. They are constantly changing, coming and going until every drop is naturally removed and just as naturally replaced many times throughout the years. Some of that water evaporates, some seeps into the aquifers, and some just drains away. In the meantime, the water in those lakes and ponds is being replenished by precipitation, by incoming seepage, and by inflowing streams.

Limnologists, or lake experts, tell us that the lakes we see today will in time disappear from the face of the earth. They will undergo a three-way change: physically, biologically, and chemically. For one thing, there's sedimentation, which is the major cause of lake disappearance. Since lakes are fed in part by incoming streams, they slowly fill up with river sediments. Then water-loving plants take root along the edges. There they grow and decay, grow and decay, until what was once a sparkling blue lake turns into a green and soggy swamp. In the end, the swamp turns into a spongy meadow, which becomes dotted with trees and ultimately turns into a shady, leaf-littered woodland.

Another cause of lake disappearance is the imbalance between inflow and outgo. In dry regions, such an imbalance is common because the rate of recharge is often slower than the rate of evaporation. Then, as the water evaporates, the lake shrinks and the water becomes salty. Utah's Great Salt Lake is now only a remnant of former Lake Bonneville. There the water is so briny that if you were to dive in, you'd float like a cork. If you were keen on speed racing, you'd drive like the wind on the Bonneville Salt Flats that border the lake.

So the centuries and the millenniums pass by. Ponds and lakes form, fill up or evaporate, then disappear. Their waters, however, do not disappear from the hydrologic cycle. Those waters that seep into the aquifers move

through the underground arc of the cycle. Those that vaporize move through the atmospheric arc. Those that
drain away to the rivers run off in the surface arc to
the ocean, from whence they are again distilled to the
atmosphere.

Now pointing out the transient nature of these waters is not meant to belittle their importance. It is merely

*Racing on the Bonneville Salt Flats. (Utah State Department of
Transportation)*

meant to call attention to two facts: that in nature nothing lasts forever, and that in the earth system, nothing is
ever lost.

Transient or not, lakes are important in the water
budget of this planet because, *at any given moment*, they
contain about fifty times as much fresh water as all
the earth's flowing streams. (See the chart on page 5.) It
was not, however, along the lake shores that civilization
developed. Throughout history, civilization developed
mostly along riverbanks—along the Nile, the Indus, the
Tigris, the Euphrates, and the great inland waterways of
China because rivers provided access to inland areas and
served as abundant, renewable sources of water for people and their fields. In the spring of the year, those sedi-
ment-laden rivers overflowed their banks and coated the
land with rich, black silt. When the waters receded, the
ancient farmers, ankle-deep in the flooded fields, planted
their rice. In time, more venturesome farmers extended
their plantings beyond the reach of the flood waters. With
crude hoes and wooden shovels, they dug little channels
from the farthest fields to the river, breached the river-
bank, started the water flowing, and in this way established the one-man-one-farm system of irrigation.

No matter how basic a river may be to the development of civilization, it is not an entity in itself and may
therefore be changed by nature or man—for better or
worse. A river is a spillway system. Even more than a
lake, it is fed by tributaries flowing from the hinterland,
by runoff draining from the hillsides, and by ground
water seeping from the aquifers. It is this continuous
inflow that keeps them running. Additionally, there are
seasonal happenings that may change a river's character
dramatically. Spring thaws and snowmelt may create racing, bubbling streams that become intermittent thready
creeks in the summer. Torrential rains and flash floods
may so increase the volume of water in a riverbed that the
river doesn't just overflow; it becomes turbulent, breaks

through its banks, and changes course altogether, leaving the old bed abandoned and dry. Years later, children on an all-day hike will pepper their scout master with questions: What happened here? Where did the river go? What made the water disappear?

Though not all turbulent rivers change course, some have, nevertheless, created serious problems for the people who depended on them for an uninterrupted supply of usable water. With the coming of this century, however, scientists and engineers learned how to anticipate and manage many river problems with new technology. Faced with an erratic river, they draw up a program that includes containment and/or regulation and/or prevention. They may contain rampaging spring waters within the riverbed with sandbags and by building the banks higher with levees and dikes. They may regulate the flow of the river by impounding surplus water in storage reservoirs behind dams, then releasing the water as needed. They may prevent flooding by restoring the forests and meadows in the drainage basin.

A now-classic example of river regulation is the one that tamed the wild Tennessee, a feat once considered impossible. This river, which drains seven states and regularly receives the heaviest rainfall along the Atlantic seaboard, once pauperized the people who lived along its banks. A really good spring thaw in the mountains would send the river cresting for miles, ripping up the adjoining fields and sometimes destroying whole towns. The water would spill into the streets, run into the basements, float the stuff that's usually stored in basements, then rise and rise until it seeped under the doors of the first-floor rooms. When the water had drenched the rugs, soaked the baseboards, and was beginning to lap the tabletops, the father would pick up a long-handled ax, climb into the attic, and chop a hole in the roof. Through this hole he would lift his family and the household pets, then scramble through himself. There, on the slippery roof, they all stayed, hoping to be rescued by a police patrol in a motorboat. And they were lucky if their house also stayed and wasn't swept off its foundation by the surging waters.

By the second half of the century, however, the Tennessee had been tamed and harnessed in the service of the state by the Tennessee Valley Authority (TVA), an agency established by President Franklin Delano Roosevelt. The TVA undertook a monstrous job of engineering and construction. It hired tens of thousands of workers, provided them with bulldozers, backhoes, explosives, electric shovels, and tons and tons of cement and steel. Their goal was to regulate the flow of that river, and they did—with some thirty dams and reservoirs, plus the necessary number of diversion canals.

Fontana Dam on the Little Tennessee River in North Carolina can produce 238,500 kilowatts of electricity. (Tennessee Valley Authority)

An aerial view of strip cropping on inclined fields, which prevents excessive runoff. (USDA—Soil Conservation Service photo by Erwin W. Cole)

The Tennessee drainage basin was so transformed that this regulated river has become a multipurpose system. Equipped with locks, it now serves as a barge-studded highway that transports millions of tons of sand and gravel for thousands of miles every year. It provides some 10,000 miles (16,093 kilometers) of shoreline for public parks and public docks for boating and fishing. It releases so much power as it plunges over the dams that it has become one of America's largest producers of low-cost hydroelectricity. Additionally, it no longer floods the countryside. Instead, it permits peaceful utilization of the adjoining land, which means more work, higher wages, and bigger profits for all concerned.

Of course, not all rivers require such expensive, large-scale engineering. Where the flooding is modest, sandbags and flood walls may be quite sufficient. And as conservationists will tell you, the best, most natural, and least expensive way to control flooding is to prevent it. Reforestation is one key; another is the adoption of improved agricultural practices, such as strip cropping, to prevent runoff. (See the photograph on page 83.)

No, rivers are not forever, as you can see by the stories of rivers that disappear from their beds or rampage over the countryside unless they are regulated. But here is another story of another river. This one wasn't at all erratic or turbulent, but rather well behaved until a part of it was made to disappear by man. This is the story of the lower Colorado River.

By the middle of this century, so much Colorado River water was being stored in Lake Meade in order to run the hydroelectric plant at Hoover Dam, and so much water was being pumped away to irrigate the farms and orchards of southern California and Arizona, and so much more was being diverted at Morelos Dam to the Alamo Canal for Mexican use, that not a single drop of water has been left in the channel below Morelos Dam since 1950. Only at the southernmost reaches downstream does the dry Colorado become a river again because its bed is intercepted by the Rio Hardy and a number of local tributaries. As a river again, the Colorado then drains into the Gulf of California.

Whether it is nature or man's mismanagement that changes the state of a lake or the course of a river, the result is the same—a dislocation of the fresh-water supply. Engineers can correct these dislocations, but they can do so only at great expense. Then? Then the cost of water rises and an aroused public demands that their government and their scientists *do something.*

Actually, the scientists are doing something. In their search for usable surface water, they found that the largest source in the world is right next door. That is the ocean, and desalination experts have learned how to process the salty ocean water and produce fresh by hundreds of thousands of gallons a day.

What's holding us back, the man in the street wants to know.

According to the scientists, only one thing—cost. As soon as they can get the cost down—and they are working on it—we will be able to have all the desalinated water we want.

7

Saline Water as a Source for Fresh Water

In this, the latter part of the twentieth century, we are learning that the salty sea is a viable new source for fresh surface water. And what a bountiful source! It covers more than 72 percent of the planet's surface and holds 97 percent of the world's water, but that water just sloshes around there. It's unfit for drinking, unfit for irrigating, and unfit for piping through industrial machinery because it is 3.5 percent salt. This computes to 35,000 parts of salt per 1 million parts of water (ppm). Compare this with the United States regulation that pegs the salt content for drinking water at 500 to 1,000 ppm.

Then there's seawater's cousin—brackish water. Great volumes of brackish water, with a salt content ranging from 0.1 percent to much more than 3.5 percent, trickle through some of the ancient aquifers. Many old-time country people are familiar with such waters, having on occasion drawn a briny brew from old wells and even from some new ones. Generally, such wells are closed down and written off as disasters. In some instances, however, they have been converted to profitable ventures. In ancient inland China, for example, where salt was scarce and consequently expensive, briny wells were deliberately developed. (See the illustration on page 88.)

Although salty seawater is taken for granted, salty well water is not. How did so much salt get down there, deep under the ground? To some extent, the rain is responsible.

Remember that rain brings with it some of the gases in the atmosphere. As it seeps through the ground, it leaches minerals out of the rocks. As the long centuries pass, the dissolved gases and minerals increase the salinity of the underground water and make the aquifers more than a little briny.

There are yet two other reasons for underground deposits of briny, or brackish, water. These are *entrapment* and *encroachment.*

Entrapment of salty water happened millenniums ago when ancient seas rippled over what is now dry land.

A Chinese brine-well drilling rig. (National Water Well Association)

During those eons, the salty waters percolated into the aquifers beneath the seabed, and most of that salty water is still there.

Encroachment is something else. It's a twentieth-century phenomenon. Encroachment is the underground intrusion of seawater, and it happens, you will recall, in densely populated coastal areas where fresh water has been pumped excessively for urban needs.

Whether brackish deposits stem from rainwater, entrapment, or encroachment, the fact remains that man has inherited saline water on the ground and under the ground, in addition to that saline water in all the oceans. Still, if we're thinking of saline water as a new source for fresh, we can blend it with fresh or we can do one of two things. We can take the salt out of the water, or we can take the water out of the salt. In either instance, we need desalination plants.

Of course, this is easier said than done. Nevertheless, progress is being made. By 1981 there were on this planet 2,200 land-based desalination plants in operation or under construction, with capacities greater than 25,000 gallons (94,625 liters) per day. And these, powered by fossil fuel or electricity, were capable of producing 7.57 million cubic meters of fresh water daily. (A cubic meter of water is equivalent to 264 gallons or 1,000 liters.)

A century ago, such desalination plants had not even been dreamed of. People relied on springs and wells and rivers and lakes for their fresh water, just as their ancestors had done before them. And all that time, sailing men had to rely on the limited number of fresh-water casks they could store in a ship's hold. Of necessity, exploration was restricted to short runs from the mainland to the nearest island, and then to the next. Always the captain and the crew worried that they might run out of drinking water. This fear was even greater than the fear of the unknown dangers on the unchartered ocean.

Not until the sixteenth century did British sailing ships, captained by such swashbucklers as Sir Francis Drake, begin roaming the Seven Seas without fretting about empty water casks, for a new word and a new process had come into their lives: *distillation.*

Distillation is a simple process whereby fresh water is removed from salt water. Nature does this all the time, as you can see for yourself. Place a glass full of seawater on a sunny windowsill and leave it there until all the water has evaporated. When that happens, you'll find a layer of salt remaining in the glass. It was solar energy that vaporized—distilled—that glassful of water, and some day, when conditions are right, that water will return to earth as snow or rain.

On Drake's ship, the distillation process was set up in

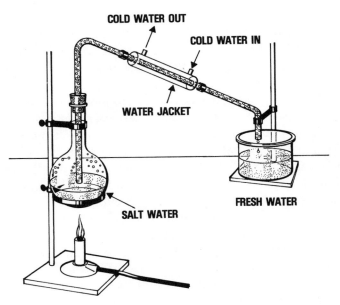

COLD WATER OUT

COLD WATER IN

WATER JACKET

SALT WATER

FRESH WATER

A distillation setup to extract fresh water from salt water. (Office of Water Research and Technology, U.S. Department of the Interior)

the ship's galley, where the cook had a brisk fire going. The water master filled an iron pot with seawater, covered it tightly, and set it to boil. As the water boiled, the steam was drawn off in a copper tube. The tube was run through a bath of cold water, which made the steam condense and drip into a little tank. And there, there was fresh water for the crew. (See the diagram above of a simple setup often used today to illustrate this process.)

In due time, more efficient distillers, called stills, were developed and installed on ocean-going warships. Today, both warships and cruise ships carry modern evaporators and produce all the water they need—as much as 200,000 gallons (757,080 liters) a day. So well known are ships' desalination capabilities that on more than one occasion, when coastal cities were hit by severe droughts, the town fathers sent out an SOS to a ship. Obligingly, the captain dropped anchor nearby, got his still going full blast, and piped welcome fresh water to the mainland.

Great strides have been made in the development of land-based stills. As early as the 1880s, a good-sized one that was constructed high in the Andes near Las Salinas saved a large mining operation from going bankrupt. This mine, superbly rich in ore, had a well nearby that was brimming with water, but it was briny water. What should be done? The men needed drinking water, as did the mules that hauled the ore, but the only potable source was miles and miles away. To save the business, a clever American engineer, a man ahead of his time, built a solar still that took the fresh water out of the brine.

This still looked like an inverted "V" with a glass roof fitted with hundreds of angled panes of ordinary window glass underneath it. Its sides rested on the ground over a large shallow basin that had a black bottom and was filled with brine pumped in from the well. Pure water, vaporized by the solar energy, condensed into droplets on the undersides of the cool glass roof and the panes, slid down the glass sides into little troughs, and was piped to a collecting tank. Voilà! The crew had all the drinking water it needed. That solar still delivered 60,000 gallons (227,124 liters) of fresh water a day—a tremendous amount when you consider the fact that, living under those rugged conditions, each of the men and each of the mules required no more than a couple of gallons a day.

By this time, you may be asking yourself the same two questions that bothered the "sidewalk superintendents" watching that solar still going up.

What about the salt, they wondered, that is left behind in the basin after the water is vaporized? The engineer's answer was that when the brine gets too concentrated, it is flushed out by the pumps.

They also wondered how the glass roof could remain cool enough to cause the vapor to *condense* with all that heat building up inside the still. The engineer explained that air currents remove heat from the top of the glass by convection. He also pointed out that after the sun's rays pass through the glass, their heat energy is absorbed by the black bottom of the basin. It is this absorbed heat that causes the water to evaporate. Then because there is a considerable difference in temperature between the cooler glass roof and the steaming vapor, water droplets condense on the cooler undersurface of the roof.

Almost a hundred years were to pass before the simple solar still that worked so well in the Chilean mountains was adapted to a plant on the Negev Desert in Israel. This was a pilot project funded by the German Federal Republic, and its purpose was not to distill fresh water to drink but to produce enough fresh water to support a *saltwater greenhouse* for the concentrated production of food in that hot and arid land.

The greenhouse, in operation since 1975, is described by Dr. Rolf Bettaque in the *Proceedings of the 6th International Symposium on Fresh Water from the Sea.* Bettaque notes that this kind of installation may be built wherever seawater, heavily mineralized lake water, or briny wells are available. On the Mideast desert, where only brackish water is available, this one was built to resemble an ordinary greenhouse except that it has a solar still integrated in its hermetically sealed twin roofs. The upper roof is made of clear window glass, the lower one of thin ultraviolet-resistant foil that's covered with a special evaporation tissue. A small plastic pump lifts brine from a nearby well first to an insulated storage tank, then to the narrow space between the roofs. Under the desert sun, this space becomes very hot, causing vapor to rise from the brine. As happened in the Chilean greenhouse, the vapor condenses and beads the underside of the cool glass roof with droplets. These droplets slide down the sides of the roof into a central collection tank, providing enough fresh water for the drip irrigation system in the greenhouse and for the personal use of the workers.

One problem troubled the technicians when the greenhouse was being constructed. That was the very real possibility that, because of the continued evaporation, a salty crust would build up on the tissue and reduce the space between the roofs. Well, a solution was found, and it proved to be as simple as it was effective. They set the pump to pipe more brine into the space between the roofs than could actually be evaporated. This surplus flushes out the tissue, then flows back to a salt-water tank and from there to the storage tank to be recycled.

In the desert this salt-water greenhouse has been maintaining acceptable temperatures year-round. There it sits, surrounded by burning sands, all the while crammed with green and flourishing plants—tomatoes, cucumbers, melons, maize, and peppers, as well as chrysanthemums that are grown for export.

Salt-water greenhouses would seem to hold great promise for the extension of agriculture, especially to hot and dry lands that border the sea. In them, year-round agriculture is no problem. In them, too, success is virtually guaranteed because, with only the desalinated water and a little fertilizer, plants grow rapidly and yield astonishing harvests. As Bettaque points out, "Salt-water greenhouses may be one of the answers to starvation and despair in many arid parts of the developing countries. Such greenhouses require no *natural* fresh water. They require little or no fossil fuel energy. They require little or no foreign aid or technological assistance. And they can be built and operated by the local people with little or no particular skill."

To describe the many kinds of solar stills that have already been tested and found operable would be impossible. It's enough to say that the concept of solar distillation, with its promise of large quantities of fresh water, has stimulated countless professionals and nonprofessionals to try their hands at inventing the ultimate still— one that would be economical, efficient, durable, and adaptable to various degrees of salinity. However, in nature, nothing is free, including desalinated water. There are capital costs and maintenance costs. Solar stills, nevertheless, have a good track record, especially in small communities where the sunshine is abundant and the local supply of fresh water is limited and/or of poor quality.

Of course, stills vary in design, in size, and in capability, but the simple basin-type has the best immediate potential. The Chilean still is an example of the basin type. The salt-water greenhouse in the Mideast is not.

Tantalizing though solar stills may be, developers interested in really large-scale commercial desalination of saline waters invariably ask what other methods there are.

A number of conversion methods are already in operation in the United States, Mexico, and some of the Caribbean countries, as well as in the Arabian peninsula, Asia, Africa, and Australia. In the main, these installations are powered by the conventional fossil fuels, which carry an escalating price tag. Of the desalination methods presently under research and development, four will be considered here. They are: distillation (the one most commonly used), crystallization, reverse osmosis, and electrodialysis.

Consider *distillation*. Simple as this setup is in the solar stills installed in Chile and the Mideast, really large plants today use a more sophisticated method, called flash distillation, for removing fresh water from ocean water or brackish deposits.

Flash distillation is based on the principle that the temperature at which water boils and vaporizes depends on pressure. At sea level, where the air pressure is 14.7 pounds per square inch (psi), water boils and flashes into steam at 212 degrees F (100 degrees C). But campers preparing their food on mountaintops know that there it takes longer for bread to bake and chicken to stew. The reason? At higher altitudes, the air is thinner and the pressure, consequently, lower. On top of Alaska's Mt. McKinley (altitude 20,300 feet or 6,187 meters), where the pressure stands at a low 56 percent of sea level pressure, water boils at 184 degrees F (84.04 degrees C). On the other hand, if you were using a pressure cooker at twice sea-level pressure, your water would not boil at 212 degrees F (100 degrees C) but at 248 degrees F (120 degrees C).

So much for the correlation between pressure and temperature in real life. Could a similar correlation be duplicated in science labs and industrial plants? Ingenious engineers, bright technicians, and creative thinkers proved that it could. And they did indeed cause water to boil and flash at *decreasing* temperatures by using a series of closed vacuum vessels, each set at a correspondingly lower pressure. In this way, they were able to boil and vaporize seawater not once, but several times, and by so doing, produced great quantities of fresh water at lower cost. Today this is called the multistage flash distillation system.

A diagram showing the flash distillation process. (Office of Water Research and Technology, U.S. Department of the Interior)

FLASH DISTILLATION

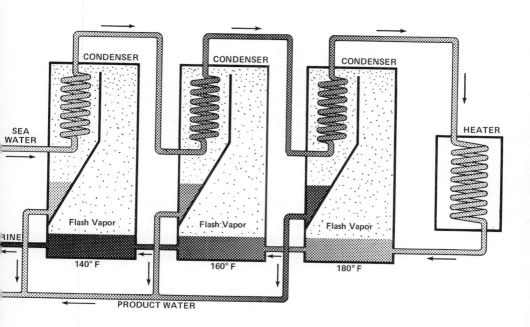

For an explanation of the way in which flash distillation works in a commercial plant, look at the diagram on page 95.

Start at the left side of the diagram where cold seawater is pumped into the first condenser, which is nothing more than a simple coil. From there, the water moves to the second and third condensers, after which it enters the heater coil and is raised to a temperature of 250 degrees F (121 degrees C). Then it moves back to the far right-hand chamber. Here, because the pressure is somewhat below normal, some of that brine boils instantly and flashes into steam. The flashed vapor then comes into contact with the cold-water condenser, whereupon it turns into pure water and runs off in a pipe to a collection tank. At the same time, the hot brine, reduced now to 180 degrees F (82 degrees C) moves on to the next chamber, where the pressure is still lower. Again it boils, vaporizes, condenses, and turns to pure water. The process is repeated in the third chamber even though the temperature of the brine is down to a low 140 degrees F (60 degrees C). There it flashes because the pressure is also low. Now notice what happens to the used still-warm brine. It is disposed of in the sea, although in some other plants it is returned to the system and recycled, thus saving on the cost of fuel for the heater.

One of the first American desalination facilities was authorized by the United States Congress in 1958. This million-gallons-a-day multistage flash distillation system located at San Diego, California, was in operation for less than two years when orders came to dismantle it and ship it to the American naval base at Guantanamo Bay, Cuba. What a hurried shipment that was because Fidel Castro was threatening to shut off the Navy's fresh-water supply. The dismantled plant arrived in Cuban waters, was assembled posthaste, and the Navy got all the desalinated seawater it needed. As for San Diego, that city was rewarded with a newer distillation plant filled with new and improved technology.

*   *   *

Crystallization is a method altogether different from distillation. Instead of heating the saline solution to the point of vaporization, this method cools it to the point of freezing, whereupon ice crystals of pure water are formed, melted, and pumped away.

One crystallization method that gets high marks from scientists is the vacuum-freezing-vapor-compression process. To understand how it works, look at the diagram below and follow the arrows.

Cold seawater is pumped into the deaerator, where it loses its air and its noncondensable gases. It then moves along to the heat exchanger, through the refrigeration unit, and into the hydroconverter as very cold brine.

Now comes the interesting action. First, because the

A diagram showing the crystallization method of converting salt water to fresh water. (Office of Water Research and Technology, U.S. Department of the Interior)

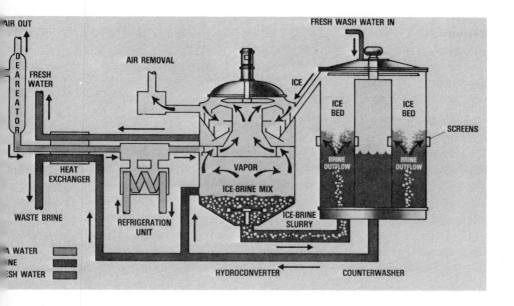

pressure is low in the hydroconverter, a portion of the seawater flashes into vapor, and since vaporization removes heat, as much as 10 percent of the brew freezes into ice crystals. These crystals slosh around in the remaining liquid and form an ice-brine slurry that's pumped to the counterwasher. Then, in the counterwasher, the crystals are compacted, rise to the top, and are washed with some of the fresh water that this plant has already produced. The saltless ice is then mechanically scraped into the upper part of the hydroconverter, where it melts into fresh water. Finally, fresh water and waste brine are both discharged. The fresh water goes to a collection tank, the remaining brine goes to the sea. In some plants, however, in order to save on energy, some of that used brine is blended with fresh seawater and sent along to the hydroconverter.

The crystallization method is a favorite with many because it requires little energy to convert seawater to fresh. It also produces very little corrosion because low temperatures are easy on the equipment. However, the process is not yet cost-competitive because refrigeration equipment is more expensive than distillation equipment.

The third conversion process, a membrane method, desalinates sea or brackish water by *reverse osmosis* (RO).

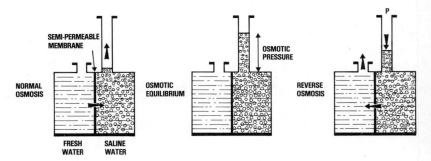

A series of three diagrams showing normal osmosis, osmotic equilibrium, and reverse osmosis. (Office of Water Research and Technology, U.S. Department of the Interior)

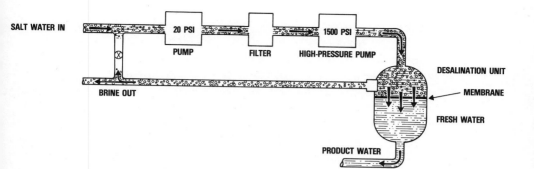

A diagram showing the reverse osmosis process used in converting salt water to fresh water. (Office of Water Research and Technology, U.S. Department of the Interior)

Osmosis itself is a common process that permits a fluid (a liquid or a gas) to pass through a selective semi-permeable membrane. In this case, the membrane doesn't permit salt to pass through. (See the illustrations on page 98.) The rectangular tanks are divided into two equal compartments by such a membrane. If there's a weak salt solution, such as tap water, on one side of the membrane and a stronger salt solution, such as seawater, on the other side of the membrane, *normal osmosis* takes place: water from the weaker solution moves automatically through the membrane into the stronger solution and dilutes it. If the system is closed, pressure builds up in the stronger solution. Such a difference in pressure between the two solutions is called osmotic pressure difference. If that difference becomes great enough, it stops the flow of water between the solutions altogether, and then a state of *osmotic equilibrium* exists.

Desalination engineers take this matter of osmotic pressure one step further. They use pumps to raise the pressure on the stronger salt solution from 20 psi to 1,500 psi. Then the osmotic flow is reversed, and pressurized water flows out of the stronger saline solution into the weaker one, leaving the salt behind.

In the reverse osmosis process, as shown in the diagram at the top of the page, the salt water is piped in and pumped through a filter, where suspended solids are removed. A second pump then raises the cleaned water to operating pressure and sends it along to the desalination unit. Here a portion of the salt water permeates the membrane and is collected as product water below. At the same time, the leftover brine, now highly concentrated, is discharged from the top of the unit to the sea or pumped back to the unit for recycling. Of course, different plants carry out the RO principle in different process designs, and many of them are somewhat more sophisticated than the one described here.

By the early 1980s, the RO process was dominant in the conversion of brackish water to fresh water in such plants as the Kashima Steel Works of the Sumitomo Metal Industries, Ltd., in Japan, which has been producing 3.5 million gallons (13.2 million liters) a day since 1975; and in Florida's City of Cape Coral, which sits on a salt-water peninsula and which has been producing 3 million gallons (11.4 million liters) a day since 1977. The use of the membrane process for seawater conversion has increased dramatically, as indicated by the installation of a 3-mgd plant in Jidda, Saudi Arabia, in 1979, and a 3-mgd plant in Key West, Florida, in 1981. And research continues briskly because reverse osmosis is such an intriguing process. It presents few scale and corrosion problems because it operates at normal temperatures. It consumes very little energy—just enough to drive the pumps. And it requires no high technological equipment other than the membrane itself.

Yet another desalination method that needs to be considered is a membrane separation process called *electrodialysis*. The oldest of the membrane processes, it too needs more research to bring the cost down.

An electrodialysis unit consists of a cell containing not one membrane, as in a reverse osmosis plant, but two. These are ion-selective membranes. An ion is an atom that has gained or lost one or more electrons. It so hap-

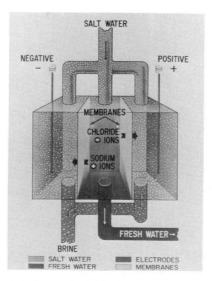

A diagram showing how electrodialysis extracts fresh water from brine. (Office of Water Research and Technology, U.S. Department of the Interior)

pens that sodium chloride (NaCl), which is common table salt and the most abundant salt in saline solutions, consists of two kinds of ions: sodium ions, which carry a positive electrical charge and are noted chemically as Na + ; and chloride ions, which carry a negative electrical charge and are noted as Cl—. In electrodialysis, one of the two selective membranes is *cation-permeable*, meaning it will allow the passage of the positive sodium ions. The other membrane is *anion-permeable*, meaning it will allow the passage of the negative chloride ions. (See the illustration above.)

In a simple electrodialysis cell, two of those permeable membranes are installed between two electrodes, one negative and one positive. (An electrode is the terminal of an electric source.) The cell is then filled with salt water, and the pumps keep that water coming. As soon as the electric current is switched on, the seawater's positive sodium ions move to the negative electrode and the negative chloride ions move to the positive electrode. What's left in the center is fresh water. The fresh water is drawn off to one side while the concentrated brine is drawn off to the other side.

Prior to the middle of this century, electrodialysis was only a lab curiosity. It began to attract commercial attention after 1954 when Saudi Arabia, needing drinking water for her oil exploration camps, installed a number of such systems. Since then, hundreds of small units that produce 25 to 30 gallons (94.5 to 113.4 liters) of fresh water a day have been installed in private homes served mainly by brackish water in the southwestern United States. These units can be leased for a few dollars a month, and you can be sure that an increasing number of homeowners in Texas, plagued by briny wells, have become enthusiastic fans of the electrodialysis process. Larger units have also been installed here and there where the water is brackish. One such is located in Coalinga, California, which used to be a coaling station on the Southern Pacific Railroad and got its water delivered by the railroad. But with its population increasing, an electrodialysis plant that each and every day produces 1,000 gallons (3,785 liters) of fresh water from brackish has been a welcome installation. Since then an increasing number of larger units producing many millions of gallons of fresh water a day have been built around the world and are in operation currently.

As we approach the end of this century, it's clear that desalination is an idea whose time has come. We have the conventional technology and the know-how, and although some engineering problems have yet to be ironed out, it is the cost factor that is most troublesome. Fossil fuels or nuclear electricity with which to run the plants are so expensive that the planning of new facilities and the construction of many already on the drawing boards may have to be postponed indefinitely. Indefinite postponement, however, need not be seen as a defeat for desalination, but rather as a holding action while plans for less-expensive technologies are devised.

One such plan captured the public fancy in 1977 when the United States and Saudi Arabia signed a Project

Agreement for Cooperation in the field of Solar Energy (SOLERAS). The purpose? To demonstrate the use of solar energy in desalting brackish water and seawater.

You wouldn't expect the Saudi Arabians, with all their oil reserves, to be interested in solar desalination. Indeed, they do use their oil to generate low-cost electricity for desalination plants all along the coast. Their desalination production figures are impressive: 87,000 cubic meters (22,968,000 gallons) of fresh water a day from the sea in 1977; 182,000 cubic meters (48,048,000 gallons) a day in 1981; and a projected 8 to 12 million cubic meters (2,113 million to 3,168 million gallons) a day for the year 2000.

But the Saudis want to develop greenhouse agriculture in their inland deserts. Great deposits of brackish water underlie these deserts, but the deposits cannot be desalinated without electricity to run the pumps and the plants, and electricity is not available in the Saudi interior because there's no network to transmit it from the coastal power plants. Additionally, the Saudis are trying to make solar energy for salt water conversion practicable before their fossil fuels run out.

What do people in the technological arena think about the future of desalination?

Wilfred Hahn, assistant director of technology development in the Office of Water Research and Technology of the United States Department of the Interior, wrote: "Historically, desalting was first used where no other source of fresh water existed—aboard ship—and where there was no economic comparison with alternative supplies. Next it was used to support highly profitable industrial activities where alternatives did not exist, as well as profitable resort and vacation sites where alternatives were undependable. In my opinion, the area of economic utilization will continue to expand. World desalting capacity has roughly doubled every three years, and I think that the future of desalting is quite promising."

8

Atmospheric Water—a Source to Be Tapped

It's to the third arc of the hydrologic cycle—the atmosphere—that scientists are now looking for additional supplies of water because the sky is a source of fresh water and there are ways to haul that water down.

There's an ocean in the sky, a complex turbulent ocean of water and air that swirls over the planet. This ocean is invisible when the water is in vapor form because both vapor and air are invisible gases. It's only when the vapor cools and condenses, as water droplets or as ice crystals, that we see this ocean. Then the clouds appear.

There are two kinds of clouds—warm clouds and supercooled clouds.

Warm clouds are above freezing—above 32 degrees F (0 degree C). They are composed of water droplets that have formed around condensation nuclei. The nuclei may be particles of dust or sea salt, or they may be combustion particles of smoke and soot from home and factory chimneys, from grass and forest fires, or from volcanic eruptions.

Supercooled clouds are composed of liquid water drops that may be as cold as minus 40 degrees F (minus 40 degrees C). When natural or artificial ice nuclei are added to them, they become ice crystal clouds. Pilots try to avoid supercooled clouds because any aircraft flying through them is sure to ice up.

With clouds we can have rain—but not always. We cannot have rain if the droplets are very small because small droplets fall so slowly and are so light that the winds catch them up and fly them about, keeping them airborne. Their failure to reach the ground is most provoking to farmers, who see their fields drying up while day after drought-stricken day mile-high cumulus clouds and flat, gray blankets of stratus clouds drift across the sky.

Long ago, when droughts occurred, people thought that only rainmakers could coax water from the clouds. Naturally, rainmakers were then held in high esteem. Using imitative magic, they would put on quite a show to justify this esteem. In one Russian village, for example, a rainmaker and two assistants would climb a leafy tree, and when they were comfortably settled in the branches, one assistant would pound his drum with a wooden mallet to imitate the crash of thunder; the other would beat a couple of burning brands to imitate the flash of lightning; and the rainmaker himself would dip a bundle of twigs into a brimming pail and sprinkle the drops around to imitate a drenching rainstorm. Did this magic work? The ancients thought it did.

In time, magic and superstition gave way to ritual and prayer. In the Western world, Indian tribes performed elaborate ceremonial rain dances, as do the Natchez and the Hopi tribes to this very day. In Macedonia and Thessaly, some Greeks, with the aid of their children, still beseech the heavenly powers to send rain. In long, flowery processions, boys and girls sing their way to the wells and springs and sprinkle the dry earth there with water from their little pails.

By the nineteenth century, however, some supposedly scientific suggestions about what makes rain began to surface. According to one, it was thunder that brought the rain. The French took to firing cannons into the sky, while the Dutch and Swiss fired guns and rockets. In 1890, in drought-seared Texas, Robert C. Dyrenforth, a general in the United States Army, set off some thunderous salvos of artillery fire. He detonated explosives on the ground and oxyhydrogen balloons in the air, and after his noisy experiments, it did indeed rain. But scientists scoffed. There's no proof, they said, that the rain which followed those activities in Texas, as well as in France, Holland, and Switzerland, was due to human intervention. It was more likely due to natural causes.

Still, the belief that human intervention could bring on rain persisted so strongly that in 1953 the United States government, by Act of Congress, established the Advisory Committee on Weather Control and charged it with looking into the possibilities of increasing precipitation in certain areas. Captain Howard T. Orville, chairman of the committee, and F. A. Berry, chief scientific adviser, soon made it their business to clarify a number of items about which innovative meteorologists, or atmospheric scientists, were troubled. For one thing, they called attention to the fact that cloud census studies showed that in a great many semiarid areas, where the land was blowing away in dusty clouds, the sky was covered with water-laden clouds much of the time. Since it was already known that clouds withhold their moisture when their water droplets are too light to fall to earth, Orville and Berry and the other committee members pondered two questions:

Can we coerce the droplets into becoming heavy enough to fall to the ground?

Can we find a way to haul down the needed moisture from the sky *when* and *where* we want it?

A hundred years ago, such questions would have made a responsible scientist laugh until his sides ached. In 1957, however, these questions were taken so seriously that the committee urged the government to authorize a National Science Foundation program of study, research, and evaluation in the area of weather modification.

Actually, interest in weather control preceded the establishment of that advisory committee by some years. It had been sparked in 1946 by Dr. Vincent Schaefer, a General Electric scientist in Schenectady, New York, who did what no man had ever done before. He flew a small plane into the top of a supercooled cloud, dropped 3 pounds (1.4 kilograms) of dry ice (CO_2) into it, then photographed the long draperies of snow that began streaming from the base of the cloud into the clear air.

What made Schaefer do such a thing? Well, it started one hot and humid July day when he was conducting aircraft icing experiments in his laboratory. Since these experiments took place in a cold chamber, which is something like a refrigerator, and since it wasn't cold enough to suit him, he hit upon the idea that dry ice would be sure to lower the temperature. In went a chunk of it, and to his amazement the chamber filled with a bluish cloud of ice crystals.

This creation of a cloud of ice crystals in the laboratory had tremendous implications for weather control. It meant that the addition of dry ice to a supercooled cloud in the atmosphere might just possibly induce that cloud to precipitate.

The General Electric staff was intrigued but cautious, as scientists usually are. They suggested more studies and more experiments, but Dr. Irving Langmuir, the most daring of them all, urged Schaefer to set his sights on an experiment with an actual cloud. Accordingly, months of study and experimentation and planning followed until all seemed to be in readiness. Finally, a two-seated monoplane was rented, a dry-ice dispenser was installed, pilot Curtis Talbot was engaged to stand by, and the waiting began. They needed a suitable cloud system to appear within a reasonable distance of the Schenectady airport.

On November 13, 1946, 4 miles (6.4 kilometers) of billowing clouds sailed into sight some 38 miles (61 kilometers) to the east, just over the Massachusetts state line. Schaefer filled his cardboard ice-cream containers with dry-ice pellets and raced for the plane. Talbot hopped in after him, and they were off. When the plane hovered over Mount Greylock at an altitude of 14,000 feet (4,267 meters) and the temperature in the supercooled clouds read 0 degrees F (−20 degrees C), Schaefer tossed out his pellets, and the first man-made snowstorm—a modest one, to be sure—became a matter of history.

Of course, more flights followed, but the one that received wide media coverage occurred some weeks later, on December 20. That day began like any other day in the laboratory, until the weather report crackled over the radio. "Snow," said the announcer. The Albany Weather Station was forecasting snow for 7 P.M. that night.

One look at the leaden sky, and Schaefer decided to go aloft. At noon, he started the first of his four runs into the gray clouds, seeding them with dry ice and a bottle of liquid carbon dioxide for good measure. Nothing much happened except for a little rain here, a drizzle there, and a few scattered snow showers that didn't quite make it to earth. By two-fifteen, however, the Schenectady area began to whiten. By evening, the snow plows were out. By morning, the householders were shoveling 8 inches (20 centimeters) of snow off their sidewalks. Still, neither Schaefer nor General Electric would claim credit for causing the snowstorm. What they did say was that under the conditions they encountered, the seeding had hastened the arrival of the storm and increased the snowfall.

Of course, snow isn't rain, and it's rain people usually think about when the subject of weather control or modification comes up. Actually, a number of seeding flights had produced some respectable quantities of rain, prompting the belief among many that to produce or enhance precipitation, all you have to do is send a seeding plane aloft. However, it is not quite as simple as that because there's a chain of precipitation that takes place in supercooled clouds before snow or rain can fall. First, ice nuclei have to be present to form ice crystals, then snowflakes. Once snowflakes are formed, they continue to absorb water from the surrounding vapor until they grow heavy enough to fall. What happens then depends on the wind, the temperature, and the humidity below. Under some conditions, it snows. Under some conditions, it rains. Under some conditions, it neither snows nor rains because the snowflakes or raindrops are swept up into a fast-moving cloud that may precipitate elsewhere. Or that same cloud may be torn to tatters by a high wind and fade out of the sky.

At this point, mention must be made of Dr. Bernard Vonnegut, another General Electric scientist, who boosted the cloud-seeding process in yet another way. Instead of using dry-ice pellets to trigger the precipitation chain in supercooled clouds, he used a metal smoke. He dissolved silver iodide in an acetone solution, vaporized the solution in a hot propane flame, and the result was smoke containing myriads of microscopic ice nuclei.

To inject that smoke into the clouds, he used a generator that was either land-based or suspended from the wings of an airplane. In either instance, in a super-cooled cloud, ice crystals formed and grew on those microscopic ice nuclei, and after that the precipitation chain took over.

The seeding of warm clouds has also been done from airplanes—with water sprays and salt solutions and salt particles. To date, though, it has proven to be of little commercial value.

By the 1950s, cloud-seeding had become a fledgling science often referred to as weather modification, and it was being favorably watched, even though most of the expert operators were running into atmospheric problems they didn't know how to anticipate or avoid. Clouds don't stand still to be measured, turbulence doesn't pause to be studied, and winds blow as they will. Tons of research data had first to be accumulated about that ever changing dynamic atmosphere. But that was to take time, creative imagination, and a technology that hadn't yet been invented.

By the 1980s, however, the picture had improved so much that it was safe to say that soon—and in science, soon may be a few years away or many—when meteorologists have learned more, they'll be able to invent more of the technology they need. With that technology, they'll try to understand such factors as wind, humidity, temperature, and pressure so that they can get on with the business of inducing rain. But a word of caution is necessary so that enthusiasms don't whirl us away. Although finding answers is what scientists are after, the answers themselves sometimes raise more questions that call for still more research and technology. No matter which way you look at it, cloud behavior is very complex, and rain enhancement, although no longer a mystery, is still very baffling.

110

Have you noticed how the vocabulary has changed? Scientists no longer even mention *rainmaking.* That word, they say, implies that people can actually *make* rain, but that isn't so. Nobody can produce water unless it's already contained in the clouds in sufficient quantity. Even then, only under certain conditions can certain things be done. We can induce the cloud water that is there to precipitate, and we can increase the capacity of a cloud to produce rain by making it bigger.

What then are we to call these ongoing weather modification activities if we don't call them rainmaking?

According to Dr. Bernard A. Silverman, Chief of the Division of Atmospheric Resources Research, Bureau of Reclamation, United States Department of the Interior, "We prefer to call these activities *precipitation management.*" Silverman, an enthusiastic, energetic meteorologist, is rarely at his desk in his Denver office. Like the clouds that race across the sky, he flies from one state to another, from one country to another. He organizes committees, sits on panels, addresses grass-roots gatherings and government agencies, and, without pause, works indefatigably for action on the weather front.

Should you be lucky enough to catch him on his rounds, it won't be long before he calls your attention to the atmosphere as a renewable and inexhaustible source of usable water.

"People don't realize," he'll tell you, "how much water there actually is in the atmosphere. At any one time, there are about 14,260 billion tons [12,936.7 billion metric tons] of water, mostly in vapor form, floating over the surface of the earth. If all of that fell to the ground, it would be enough to cover the entire planet with 1 inch [2.5 centimeters] of water. But Mother Nature doesn't work that way. She cycles the water continuously—evaporating it from land and water bodies, creating clouds with it, and then returning it to us very unevenly in the form of rain and snow. The amount of precipitation that falls around the world may range from less than .1 inch

[.254 centimeter] per year in some deserts to more than 900 inches [2,286 centimeters] per year in the tropics. Some areas, such as much of the American West, don't receive enough water to support their growing populations. And so we have water shortages."

How would he help to correct those shortages?

"By precipitation management with a dependable cloud-seeding technology. The time is coming," said Silverman, "when we may be able to use such a technology to increase rain and snowfall *whenever* additional water is needed *and* suitable cloud conditions occur. The additional water can [then] be used to help increase soil moisture to grow crops and to help fill reservoirs that supply water to semiarid croplands, river basins, and thirsty cities."

What a tantalizing glimpse of things to come: atmospheric water so managed that it adds to the freshwater supply of a thirsty nation. "But"—again Silverman qualifies the situation—"we're not there yet. At this time, in the early eighties, the challenge lies in determining how and which clouds can be seeded to obtain predictable, desirable results. At this time, our job is to drive ahead with well-managed, well-planned research and development programs so that we get the results—increased water supplies—that we are out to achieve."

In fact, a sizable number of programs investigating clouds, cloud physics, and weather modification have been developed in many countries since the middle of the century. As you might expect, the first one in the United States was developed by Schaefer. That was Project Cirrus, so called because cirrus is the name of those supercooled clouds that are composed of ice crystals. The year was 1947, and the time was right. World War II was over, science was becoming important in the public mind, and the government began awarding dozens of contracts annually for the study of weather control.

A 1979 report published by the National Oceanic and Atmospheric Administration (NOAA) shows the diversity of these American studies. It describes fifty-four projects based on the use of crushed dry ice and silver iodide particles. Covering a target area of 123,880 miles square, these projects include:

- 33 that were designed to enhance precipitation and thereby increase rain, snowfall, and the depth of the snowpack;
- 7 that were engaged in efforts to alleviate hail, which periodically destroys farm crops;
- 9 that focused on fog dispersal at airports; and
- 7 that were concerned with research testing and evaluation.

As you would expect, these projects varied in size. They covered target areas ranging from 3 miles square to 25,520 miles square, and they are scattered across the

Weather charts help Project Skywater plan cloud-seeding operations. (Bureau of Reclamation)

United States from Alaska to Florida and from Delaware to California.

This may sound impressive, but the record shows that the number of states with weather-modification activities peaked in 1975 and dropped sharply in 1979. The record also shows that only about 7.5 percent of the area of the United States has so far been served by these activities.

One of the largest of the American programs is the prestigious Denver-based Project Skywater. Under the aegis of the Bureau of Reclamation, it was started in 1962 and has been going for two decades. Its staff and contractors include an exciting crew of professionals: meteorologists, physicists, chemists, technicians, computer analysts, and airplane pilots, as well as experts from business firms, colleges, and government agencies. All are high ranking, with a job to do. In field and laboratory, the scientists study weather conditions and cloud mechanics in order to be able to recognize the conditions best suited for seeding. In addition, they look for correlations between drifting clouds and open plains, forests, mountains, semiarid regions, deserts, and river basins. When not flying, the men and women on the project spend much of their time calibrating their instruments so they can better measure the properties of the clouds and their environment. How many measurements do they record in a year? Millions—so many that powerful computers must be used to process and store them.

Of the special programs that make up Project Skywater, perhaps none are more important than those that zero in on the different kinds of cloud systems. Some study the seeding of winter clouds over mountain areas. Here the idea is to find out to what extent such seeding might increase the depth of the snowpack, its water content, and its subsequent runoff, in the summer. The Five-Year Colorado River Basin Pilot Project showed an estimated potential increase of 10 percent in resultant runoff. And the

Thin streams of silver iodide trail from the wings of a cloud-seeding plane. (National Oceanic and Atmospheric Administration)

Sierra Cooperative Pilot Project, conducted over the Sierra Crest at elevations above 4,000 to 5,000 feet (1,219 to 1,524 meters), is expected to produce a similar increase when seeding operations begin.

What's so important about runoff? Well, in California's Central Valley, it could support 100,000 acres (40,000 hectares) of irrigated cropland; or if passed through a hydroelectric turbine, it could generate 60 million kilowatt hours of electricity—equal to the energy provided by 107,000 barrels of oil.

There is also the seeding of summer clouds, conducted as part of HIPLEX, the High Plains Cooperative Program. This program covers the land stretching from Montana to Texas, selected because it is underlain in part by the Ogallala Aquifer, which, as previously noted, has begun to worry hydrogeologists, who continue to warn that it may be depleted before the year 2000. Such a situation would, of course, bankrupt the farmers.

Enter HIPLEX, charged with the responsibility of developing cloud-seeding activities to increase summer rainfall. If rainfall were increased by just 1 or 2 inches (2.5 or 5 centimeters) during the growing season, incomes would be boosted by hundreds of millions of dollars a year.

Voluminous data concerning clouds and cloud conditions have been gathered, but the results haven't been summarized yet. It has become known, however, that the *timing* of additional rainfall on thirsty land is as important to the crops as the *amount* that may be induced by seeding.

In 1981, HIPLEX merged with another program called CCOPE—the Cooperative Convective Precipitation Experiment—which is based in Miles City, Montana. This, the largest field research ever mounted, concerned itself with the processes that create convective clouds, those active windblown clouds that sweep across the High Plains bringing rain and, occasionally, hail. Seeding was not part of the CCOPE plan. Instead, the scientists were to focus on cloud observations and try to improve their ability to predict precipitation and severe weather.

When American and foreign scientists converged on Miles City in May of 1981, they measured conditions on the ground and at various levels of the atmosphere. They

A build-up of cumulus clouds in the late afternoon in the Flagstaff, Arizona, area. These summertime convective clouds are being studied in connection with cloud-seeding experiments. (Bureau of Reclamation photo by E. E. Hertzog)

recorded temperature, humidity, and precipitation with a satellite-linked network of automated ground-weather stations—125 of them—some even solar-powered. They operated an interconnected system of eight radar units that noted weather events and flew fourteen instrumented aircraft to measure atmospheric conditions.

So up to date was this technology that a number of planes even carried on-board equipment that collected up to 1,800 atmospheric measurements a minute. Three months later, this portion of the experiment was completed, and then two years were set aside for the collation and interpretation of data, which is expected to boost meteorological know-how.

Evident at this time, too, was worldwide interest in atmospheric moisture as a new source of usable water. The USSR was engaging in a weather-modification program that was said to be three or four times as extensive as America's. Significant progress was also reported from Australia, Argentina, France, Germany, Canada, Switzerland, Kenya, and the Canary Islands, Spain. But the really good news came from the World Meteorological Organization (WMO), a specialized agency of the United Nations operating out of Geneva, Switzerland. Prior to 1975, the WMO had concerned itself primarily with noting cloud-seeding reports, sent in by weather-modification researchers around the world, and keeping its member nations informed. And, one by one, the member nations began to appreciate the possibilities and benefits of what the researchers were attempting to do: induce precipitation, disperse fog at airports, reduce hail damage on farm fields, and quench forest fires.

Although the WMO had from time to time been considering the organization of a central weather modification program, nothing much was done until 1975 when PEP, the Precipitation Enhancement Program, got the green light. The field site was chosen—the Duero River Basin in Spain—and that country began preparing the necessary facilities. It refurbished hangar and office space, constructed laboratories and workshops, and built a photographic darkroom and a canteen (where the chef served such excellent pescada española, manzanas en dulce, and curros that the PEP crew awarded him a cinco estrellas rating).

As the program got underway, the participating countries began contributing their specialized weather observing systems. American pilots delivered their Queen Air aircraft. Soviet engineers erected their radar system. Canadian operators installed their radar digitizer. French photographers set up their time-lapse/all-sky cameras. Spain, the host country, assumed responsibility for monitoring her radiosonde, her synoptic (forecasting) laboratory, and her nineteen-station pluviograph, or raingraph, network. And there was more as other countries joined the PEP program.

Will this worldwide effort succeed? Well, why shouldn't it? Other scientific ventures, first thought to be impossible dreams, have within this very century become world-shaking realities. Furthermore, since meteorologists have learned how to induce rain to fall from suitable clouds, why not expect them to learn how to steer rain clouds in from the ocean? The ocean, you will recall, covers almost three-fourths of the plant's surface and is the repository of most of the world's rainfall.

All in all, weather-control programs promise enormous benefits. Additionally, they cost little to operate because they require no test plants and no production facilities. So hope runs high in the Duero River Basin as scientists study the suitability of that Spanish site. Still, this is only Phase 3 of the experiment. Future plans are subject to change, and precipitation management continues to be a very complex business.

Complex or not, private rainmaking companies have been flying cloud-seeding planes wherever clients are ready to pay. Many customers are satisfied; others are disappointed when no rain falls or when so much more falls than they'd bargained for that they are deluged. Few, if any, ever complained because the service is cheap—less than five cents a cloud-seeded acre—and because no hard-and-fast guarantees are given. Those who do complain are not customers but neighbors who live some distance downwind. To them it is clear that forced precipitation upwind robs those living downwind of the rain or snow they would otherwise receive.

You can be sure that more than one battle against the "rainrobbers" has been carried into the courts, but invariably nothing comes of them. The judges simply haven't enough scientific evidence to find the rainmakers guilty beyond a reasonable doubt. And the situation has been further confused by early studies that showed that, on the average, only about 5 or 10 percent of the water vapor available for precipitation normally falls to the ground as precipitation. The remaining 90 or 95 percent moves downwind, still in vapor form. So the operators continue to argue that they aren't robbing anyone because there's plenty of moisture left up there.

A number of cases, however, kept coming up against not only private companies but also government agencies. In 1977, Idaho, which is downwind from the state of Washington, threatened to sue the latter for incalculable damages, but again nothing came of it. And note: although tempers run high when a downwind area thinks it is being robbed of rain, tempers run even higher when the same area thinks it is being rained out and flooded as a result of a cloud-seeding operation. Today, the thinking about seeding effects downwind is still inconclusive, and studies are continuing.

In the meantime, wherever cloud-seeding experiments are going on, the public is pushing for protective legislation. It is calling for the licensing of only highly trained operators. It is asking that these operators be required to obtain permits, file environmental impact statements, keep records, and be properly insured against inadvertent damage.

Still, one thing is certain. If weather modification is

looked upon only as a drought-relief activity, then little is gained, except momentarily. It's true, of course, that rain may be induced. It's true that the fields may get wet and even soaked, but that would be all. The water table would not be likely to rise—appreciably or permanently—the aquifers wouldn't be recharged, and the river levels would remain more or less the same. For weather modification

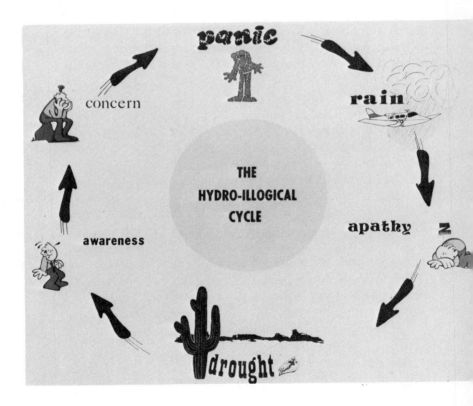

The Hydro-Illogical Cycle. The public frequently demands weather modification as a desperation measure when drought is followed by awareness, then concern, then panic. If the clouds are seeded and rain induced, then the public quickly becomes apathetic again. (The American Meteorological Society. Diagram by Bernard Silverman)

to be effective, it needs to be synonomous with year-round precipitation management. If it isn't, then as soon as the next drought strikes, the same people will again panic and will again cry for a bout of cloud-seeding. And they will only perpetuate what Silverman calls "The Hydro-Illogical Cycle." (See the illustration on page 120.)

To quote him again, "There may be no one best solution to the water problems in the United States and in the other countries of the world, but wait. When precipitation management is further developed and refined, it will be at the forefront of the technologies that help us to increase our supply of fresh water."

Of course, there are problems—scientific, ecological, economic, and legal. But these, too, will pass away. With clever meteorologists, engineers, chemists, and physicists on the job, who knows—when the twenty-first century rolls around, atmospheric water may be both a manageable resource and an affordable reality for you and me.

9

Managing Water Sources for Quantity and Quality

If you could peer into a crystal ball and ask where the water that serves our communities comes from, you'd see great quantities being pumped from aquifers under the ground and being piped by gravity flow from mountain lakes and rivers into storage reservoirs. You'd also see other reservoirs impounding flood waters for later release to rivers during dry spells. You'd even see some water being hauled down from seeded clouds and some being distilled from salty seas. One look at those brimming reservoirs and you'd brush aside the doomsayers with their cries of shortage and woe.

But if you asked the crystal ball how the people of this well-watered planet will fare in the future, you just might be jolted. You might see those people trying desperately to make do with reservoirs that are filling up with sediment, hydrants that are delivering at half capacity, farmlands that are becoming ever more salt-encrusted, and rivers so polluted that the bottled-water industry charges more for a gallon of drinking water than service stations charge for a gallon of gasoline.

Both a magical crystal ball or, more to the point, a computerized readout based on scientific research might offer the same prediction, and both might even be correct. The reason? Poor management of the water supply.

When people talk about water management, they generally picture floods and higher dams, or droughts and deeper wells. But good water management is more than that. It is responsible, long-range planning for the development and operation of resources that are known or are yet to be discovered and the utilization of the supply in terms of efficiency, selective quality, and economy.

Good management programs have a hard time getting off the ground. People are inclined to pooh-pooh such plans as long as their swimming pools are full, their lawn sprinklers are playing, and their kitchen taps spurt water as needed. When a water shortage does hit a community, they blame the weather, the sunspots, or their greedy neighboring states. If the shortage continues, they drill deeper wells, and if the wells turn out to be briny, they holler, engage in political maneuvering, and let the devil take the hindmost.

Now a combination of apathy, indiscriminate blame, and politics can result in a kind of chaos that stymies even the smartest hydrologists, engineers, and economists. Such a situation suggests an old story. Four gentlemen—a doctor, a priest, an engineer, and a politician—were discussing professions. The question was raised, "What is the oldest profession in the world?"

Said the doctor, "When God created Adam and took one of his ribs to create Eve, He performed a surgical operation, so I would say that makes medicine the oldest profession in the world."

"Not so," said the priest. "Before He created Adam and Eve, He created the world, so it's clear that the study of God and His ways—the study of religion—is the oldest profession."

"I disagree," said the engineer. "The Bible states that in the beginning there was chaos. Now, who but the professional engineers could bring order out of chaos?"

"Ah," said the politician, "but who do you think created the chaos?"

In the early 1980s, political chaos prevailed wherever ongoing water problems were permitted to exist. In the United States House of Representatives, for example, it wasn't at all unusual for one or another of the Arizona congressmen to rise and demand more funds for more dams and reservoirs for his glorious state. Population was increasing. Tourism was booming. He demanded the state's legal share of Colorado River water.

In California, harried lawmakers gathered in the state legislature. More dams for Arizona would mean the withdrawal of more water from the Colorado. That would be great for Arizona, but what about California? Was its southern region to be left high and dry? Was Los Angeles to go on water rations? Was the Imperial Valley to become a desert again?

And so the elected officials of southern California proposed a one-billion-dollar Peripheral Canal that would tie into the California Aqueduct below Sacramento and carry water from the rainy north all the way to southern parts of the state.

To this proposal more than one embattled leader in the Sacramento area shouted, "No! Water diverted from our river into such a canal would turn the Sacramento Valley into a wasteland."

Whichever way you look at it, without responsible management of the supply, water wars are sure to flare up whenever increased use threatens to rob the other fellow or drain the resources. Look at the entire United States. Although this country is water-rich in the Northeast and Northwest but water-poor in the Southwest, the average daily use per capita is 2,000 gallons (7,571 liters). Here's how this amount is disposed of. Approximately 87 gallons (329 liters) go for personal needs such as bathing, flushing toilets, washing clothes and dishes, and watering lawns and gardens. Another 2 gallons (7.6 liters) go for drinking and cooking. Yes, 2 gallons is all we require to stay alive. Most of the remainder goes to farm fields and industries, which literally gulp water. It takes 120 gallons (453.2 liters) to put an egg on your breakfast table; 35,000 gallons (132,489 liters) to produce a steak for your dinner; and 60,000 gallons (227,124 liters) to process a ton of steel for that car you're planning to buy. The water that goes into growing a steer could float a naval destroyer.

Now, 2,000 gallons (7,571 liters) per person per day would seem to be enough for our needs, but actually it isn't. Thirty-seven percent (which is almost two-fifths) of the public water that's funneled daily through the nation's water pipes to farms and cities is lost along the way, drains into the ground, and is, consequently, not available for our immediate use: about 20 percent leaks out through aging pipes, and about 17 percent is lost by evaporation from reservoirs and irrigation canals and by seepage through unlined irrigation channels. No wonder a prolonged drought creates consternation. No wonder that some water superintendents have to petition neighboring water districts for the partial loan or the temporary lease of a river, a lake, or a reservoir.

There's no question about it—we need to husband the water we have so it's available for our use. Our life style requires tremendous quantities of water. As for the arid and semiarid Third World countries, where the daily consumption of water is minimal, only access to equally tremendous quantities would give them, too, the chance to attain to the good things that spell twentieth-century progress. However, even the most careful husbanding of the usable supply cannot of itself guarantee a fine, water-based life style because it's a fact that with the good things of civilization come the bad things: pollution of the surface and subsurface waters, the severe draw-down of the water table, and frequent intrusions of deep-seated brine. Clearly then, water problems fall into two categories: one involves quantity, the other quality. And quality has to be managed just as much as quantity.

It's doubtful that quantity will be a problem in the twenty-first century. By that time, scientists will have learned how economically to haul enough water down from the sky and how to process enough from the sea and the saline rivers and the brackish reserves in order to fill our reservoirs and recharge our aquifers. And with improved management practices, they will be able to maintain the water systems so that very little is lost by evaporation and leakage.

The matter of water quality, though, is something else because it may vary from wholesome to horrible. According to an ancient anonymous poet, "Only pure love is better than pure water." But a modern scientist will tell you that pure water that is distilled and therefore devoid of necessary minerals is not good for your health. He might also quote W. H Auden, the British poet, who wrote, "Thousands have lived without love, not one without water."

Although we live in a scientific century, it's a fact that almost half of the world's population does not have easy access to good-quality water. Many live in the developing countries and have to share their water source with their animals. Those who live in urban areas modern enough to be served by a public water supply have another problem—waste-water disposal. Even so fine a city as Bangkok has no adequate sewer system. In many

Waste water standing in the streets of a city in the Middle East that has no public sewer system. (Daniel A. Okun)

A woman in Kenya collects water for her family while animals share the same source. (UNICEF photo by Arild Vollan)

cities of the Third World, cesspools and septic tanks back up, flood the streets, and contaminate the water supply with infectious viruses.

Are you wondering how you can be sure about the quality of *your* drinking water? You can be reasonably sure if the public water supply in your community is properly treated in a waterworks.

However, only since the latter part of the nineteenth century have we been served by public waterworks—facil-

ities that start with raw water and process it to make it safe. Prior to that time, it was generally believed that running rivers could take care of pollution by diluting it. This gave rise to the common notion that "dilution is the solution to pollution." And it is, when pollution is minimal.

The scientific treatment of polluted water is a modern phenomenon. It began in 1790 with Hollander Tobias Lowitz, a professor of chemistry at the Russian Imperial Academy. Lowitz read a paper at a meeting of the Economic Society of St. Petersburg that brought him a standing ovation from his colleagues for demonstrating how powdered charcoal can deodorize pungent brandy, can remove bad tastes and odors from water, and can even prevent them from forming. Subsequently, he was to earn the everlasting gratitude of seafarers for showing how charcoal filters can keep water fresh and tasty in kegs even during long ocean voyages.

Have you noticed how, right up to the nineteenth century, interest in water quality centered only on its color, taste, and odor? As long as these factors were under control, everybody was satisfied. Nobody, it seemed, had any inkling that water might contain invisible viruses and harmful bacteria. And only a few thought that the water from such rivers as the English Thames and the German Rhine, both of which flowed past heavily industrialized towns, was anything but a distasteful nuisance, a necessary concomitant of progress. Samuel Coleridge, poet and critic, was one of those few, and he expressed his sentiments in no uncertain terms when, after a visit to the unsanitary Rhine, he wrote:

> In Köln, a town of monks and bones,
> And pavements fang'd with murderous stones
> And rags, and hags, and hideous wenches;
> I counted two and seventy stenches,
> All well-defined, and several stinks!
> Ye nymphs that reign o'er sewers and sinks,
> The river Rhine, it is well known,
> Doth wash your city of Cologne;
> But tell me nymphs, what power divine
> Shall henceforth wash the river Rhine?

Washing the Rhine so it would no longer offend or be a health hazard was a management project for the distant future. Much research and even more political haranguing were to precede such an achievement.

The first breakthrough in the understanding of what it is that affects water quality came in 1853 with the onslaught of an epidemic. Cholera struck London, shut the shops, and silenced the mills. Hardly a family was spared. Daily, the death carts rattled over the cobbled streets collecting corpses from rich homes, poor homes, backyards, and gutters. Thousands died and more thousands were left debilitated for life. But then an amazing bit of news began to spread through the town. One section of London had been spared. One section was reporting no cholera deaths. One section was untouched. It seemed like magic or a special dispensation from the Lord. Yet it was neither. It was the quality of the water supply that made the difference between life and death.

What quality? How quality?

Well, at that time, cholera-struck London was being served by a number of companies that took their water from the Thames where the sewers emptied into the river. The companies did not even filter the filthy stuff. They merely pumped it to standpipes located at street intersections and in courtyards and alleys. Even so, the supply was limited to alternate days and none at all on Sundays, so you can imagine the water shortages and the state of sanitation in that city. But the untouched area that had been bypassed by the plague was served by the Lambeth Water Company, which had its intake pipes located above Teddington Weir, above the reach of London's outpouring sewer mains.

To Dr. John Snow, a Yorkshire-born physician, this was the tipoff. To him it was clear that there was some harmful substance in the polluted river water that was not present in the upland water. Snow, who was considered something of an oddball, if not a downright medical infidel, by the other practitioners, now used the London-Lambeth situation to research his thesis, which differed from his colleagues'. According to *them*, cholera started in the lungs after a person had breathed in the bad, foul, miasmic air that rose spontaneously over the garbage dumps and swamps. According to *him*, cholera attacked the digestive tract after a person swallowed that invisible, unknown substance, which he, Snow, believed was present in the dirty water.

To support his thesis, Snow reasoned that this unknown substance affected the alimentary canal in such a way as to bring on the familiar symptoms of cholera: excessive diarrhea and vomiting, followed by severe dehydration, thickened blood, difficult circulation, impaired breathing, and chills, until finally intensified cramps led to a horrible death.

Then, as an able medical man, Snow set out to investigate the area of London that had suffered the most. He called at every house there, only to find that some were being served by the London water companies, some—as close as next door—were being served by the Lambeth Water Company. But he also found that the death toll from cholera was fourteen times higher among those who had been supplied with water containing the sewage of London than it was among the Lambeth consumers, who received clean upland water.

Was Snow hailed as a pioneer by his colleagues? Not at all. He was accused of being against sanitation inasmuch as he did not seem to concern himself with the miasmas over the dumps. Not the least deterred, Snow advised and continued to advise the use of clean sources for drinking water.

This good advice was challenged the following year when some seven hundred victims were carried off in an outbreak of cholera in London's St. James Parish. This tiny, inner-city community was taking its water from its own Broad Street well, which was reputed to be filled with the purest and tastiest water in the area. But since this well was a good distance from the dirty Thames River, where was this contamination Snow had talked about coming from?

Again he investigated. He found that the deaths clustered in the vicinity of the Broad Street well. He also found that of the seventy men who worked in the local brewery and drank only the free beer there, not a single one had died, while nine mechanics who patronized a nearby coffee shop and drank the water that was served to them there succumbed and never returned. Then he discovered that a cholera-stricken baby had died at 40 Broad Street shortly before the outbreak of the epidemic. Sleuthing around, he noticed some discolored soil. He followed the discolored trail, which ran from number 40's cesspool to the well, and he concluded that the deadly seepage had entered the well and contaminated the water.

Still, the deaths continued, but what could Snow do? Tell the people to stop drinking that well water because it was deadly? Who would believe him when his colleagues wouldn't? Then luck was with him. He called on the Local Board of Guardians and was able to persuade them to remove the handle of the pump that served the well. As if by magic, the epidemic ceased.

Such patient medical detective work at a time when nothing was known about microbes! Only later was the French chemist Louis Pasteur to prove that specific microbes were responsible for specific diseases, thus disproving the theory that cholera is caused by spontaneous generation from bad miasmas. In 1884, the German doctor Robert Koch actually identified the cholera bacillus, a tiny organism that is short and thick and shaped like a comma, which he found in the bodies of cholera victims in Calcutta, India. At the same time, Koch proved that this "comma" bacillus attacks only the person who swallows it! That was what Snow had been saying.

This story of scientific detection was not to be told for about a century, not until 1966, when Norman Longmate's book, *King Cholera: The Biography of a Disease*, was published by Hamish Hamilton. It is a most dramatic story, and when you read it, you'll find yourself following Snow on his rounds, as if you were there—not that you'd ever want to be there, however.

To return to St. James Parish and the deadly water in the Broad Street well. This time Snow's reports were listened to by the London authorities, and as soon as they understood that cesspools could harbor virulent diseases, they passed a new sanitation law. Henceforth, as prescribed, no domestic waste was to go into cesspools or privies. Instead, it was to be discharged into the city's storm-sewer system, which connected with the river.

So far so good. But you cannot fool around with Mother Nature. So much domestic waste was run into the Thames that it quickly changed from being a river of water plus sewage to being a river *of* sewage. In this mass of filth, algae and bacteria increased, consumed the oxygen in the water, and caused the fish and other marine life to die, decay, and smell. So much for water quality! The smell became so unbearable that the members of the English Parliament had to have their windows covered with draperies soaked in chloride of lime.

Reports continued to come in connecting polluted river water with infectious happenings. A now-classic case occurred in Germany. There, the cities of Hamburg and Altona took their water from the Elbe River. Hamburg poured its sewage into the river but pumped its drinking water from a point several miles upstream. Altona lay downstream, seven miles below the inflow of Hamburg's waste. You'd think then that when cholera struck in 1892, Hamburg, using upstream water, would be safe, and Altona would be in trouble, but it didn't work out that way. Altona, aware of the heavy pollution throughout the Elbe, filtered its water, while Hamburg, feeling safe, took it raw. What was the result? In Hamburg, 1 out of every 71 persons succumbed, but in Altona, with its filters, only 1 out of every 286 succumbed.

So it became clear to most suppliers of public water that upland water sources were usually, but *not* always, free of infectious diseases, and that filtration was a must because water was now known to be a carrier of some diseases.

Shortly, after that, chemists in their laboratories

made a tremendous discovery. They found that chlorine—the chemical in Clorox that whitens your laundry—can effectively control infectious diseases. Immediately, some water specialists ran studies at the reservoirs, analyzed those studies, and made a startling pronouncement: "With chlorine and filtration, drinking water could be made safe, no matter how polluted the source—river, lake, spring, or well—might be."

This daring assertion, made in the early 1900s, had a profound effect. It prompted Jersey City to be the first in the United States to chlorinate its water supply, and other cities and towns quickly did likewise. To the sites of newly planned waterworks, they sent teams of state sanitary engineers and municipal engineers, consulting engineers, and bustling budget directors. In short order they worked up blueprints, commandeered bulldozers, backhoes, and cement mixers. They hired laborers and supervised the construction of some of the world's greatest public waterworks. And they contrived to provide safe drinking water for the people because in those waterworks they virtually wiped out the infectious diseases that are bacteriological in origin.

Today there are thousands of such public waterworks serving towns and cities in the industrialized countries, but thousands more are still needed all over the world.

But there are waterworks and waterworks, as you will see in the next chapter. You will also see why, in this chemical age, even the best facilities cannot by themselves solve the water-quality problems that may surface in any given region.

10

About Waterworks and Treatment Plants

In the second half of this century, innovative construction corporations changed course. Instead of building a house here and a skyscraper there, they designed and created whole new towns, such as Reston in Virginia, and whole new developments, such as Levittown in New York. High on their list of civic responsibilities was the provision of a two-way public water system that would supply the residents with a sufficiency of safe, high-quality water for their needs and relieve them of the used water by disposing of it in ways that would not harm the environment.

Understandably, the water systems in older towns had never been preplanned like that. They just grew as the towns grew. Sometimes when the water quality became noticeably degraded, public clamor caused the construction of a waterworks, and when waste water became a nuisance, more clamor caused a few more miles of sewer line to be laid. On the whole, though, the public was generally satisfied just to see a new waterworks going up.

Waterworks are scientific marvels. All use the same basic processes which start with the raw supply in rivers, lakes, springs, and wells. This often contaminated water is piped into the local waterworks and put through the customary purification processes, and there's safe drinking water.

But is it really safe? Some would say, "Most assuredly." Others would have their doubts.

Here are three examples of water facilities that were in excellent operating condition in the early 1980s:

One is in the town of Newburgh, New York, in an area that is not subject to much industrial or agricultural contamination. This is a modest filtration plant designed to fight bacterial pollution in the raw water it draws from Lake Chadwick.

The second is in the Santa Clara Valley Water District in California. It is designed to manage its water from all sources in an integrated and comprehensive program.

The third is in Fountain Valley, California. It is a water reclamation facility named Water Factory 21. The largest of its kind in the world, "21" fights not only bacterial pollution but also chemical contamination.

By appointment, Jesse Haffen, a lively, open-faced waterworks veteran in shirt sleeves and slacks, met this author at the door of the Newburgh filtration plant. Haffen, the former chief operator, now retired, serves as president of the New York Rural Water Association, but he bounces around as though he had never left this place where he had worked for so many years. Heading enthusiastically for nearby Lake Chadwick, he explained that the water treatment starts there, with monitoring for algal growth. "If the algal count gets too high, it will clog the filters. Then the algae will use up so much oxygen that the water will begin to smell bad and taste worse."

It was hard to keep up with Haffen as he plowed ahead to show off the works. "Look—there in the lake. See those fellows in the rowboats? See the brown burlap bags they're towing? There's copper sulphate in those bags. It dissolves in the water and inhibits the growth of algae. We also have an aeration unit, in that little building on the shore. We run it every once in a while so the dissolved oxygen (DO) stays at a satisfactory level in the summer and keeps the water from freezing in the winter."

A 24-inch (61-centimeter) main carries the water from the lake to the mixing basins in the outdoor portion of the waterworks. Since this main is screened at the intake point, it catches the physical debris: sticks and stones, clumps of algae, leaves, branches, fish and frogs. At the mixing basins, technicians add three chemicals to the water: chlorine, to kill bacteria; powdered activated carbon, to adsorb odors; and alum, to cause the formation of flocs—jellylike smidgens to which bits of dirt and minuscule creatures will adhere.

Dislodging the sludge build-up at the settling basin so it can be scraped and piped to the dewatering lagoons at the Town of Newburgh, New York, filtration plant

Haffen pointed to the three flocculation tanks, where millions of churning flocs resembling nothing less than an underwater snowstorm grow in size and weight as they flow to the settling basin. There they drift to the bottom and form a dark sludge, which is scraped into hoppers and piped to the dewatering lagoons.

Now the remaining water is clearer—clear enough to be pumped indoors to the filtering room. Here, red lights blink, automated machines hum, and pumps switch on and off with such a clatter that you have to shout to be heard. Here, too, are the catwalks—metal grates that rattle and clank underfoot as the water, with only a whiff of chlorine, races into the channels leading to two filter beds the size of swimming pools. Each bed holds an 11-inch (27.5-centimeter) layer of sand that's underlain by a flat plate of porous Carborundum. The water filters through the sand, drains out of the porous plate, and rushes into another noisy channel on its way to the clear-water well—an underground cistern with a capacity of 170,000 gallons (643,518 liters). Before it reaches the well, however, a resident chemist dips up some samples for analysis. He does this every once in a while to make sure that the water, which is now clean and odor-free, is also safe to drink. Based on the analysis, a control-room operator sets the chemical feeders in order to correct the chemical composition of the water. If he finds that the feeders need to be serviced, he slips into his safety gear—a shiny black rubber suit, plus goggles and mask. He also checks the waist-high eye-bubble fountain because he'll be dealing with some harsh chemicals. Once the feeders are programmed, they release just the right amount of sodium hydroxide (an alkali found in many homes under the name of caustic soda or Drano).

"This will neutralize the water and improve the taste," said Haffen, noting that the water is acidic because of the alum that had been stirred into the outdoor mixing basins. "The feeders will also release additional chlorine to kill off some of the remaining bacteria." After that, the water is judged safe to drink. It flows into the clear-water well, and from the well, it is pumped into the distribution system for use by the townspeople.

Is it safe to drink? Lawrence Goodrich, chief operator of the Newburgh plant, who accompanied us on the indoor tour, said, "For very good reasons, we cannot ever be certain that treated water is really safe to drink." Goodrich, a neat, soft-spoken, thoughtful young man, prowls the facility constantly, checking everything. He even lifts the trapdoor leading to the clear-water well and climbs down the metal wall ladder to monitor the sediments that accumulate there on the walls, bottom, and pipes. "The reason I question the safety of the water that's processed through a filtration plant such as ours, which is like most others in this country, is that water contamination isn't what it used to be in the early 1900s."

Haffen explained, "Then it was mostly bacterial coming from human and animal waste and decayed plant refuse. Bacteria, of course, are easily killed with chlorine. It was chlorine and filtration, you know, that wiped out cholera and typhoid fever and other waterborne diseases.

"Even so," said Goodrich, "we are beginning to hear that chlorine in the water is responsible for the formation of trihalomethanes, such as chloroform, and chloroform seems to be carcinogenic. It may be responsible for an increased risk of developing colon, rectal, or bladder cancer. . . . In addition, we have these thousands of new chemicals that *don't* respond to chlorine." Goodrich was referring to those new synthetic organic chemicals that had been developed by the industries since World War II and about which Dr. Daniel Okun has written so extensively.

Okun, Kenan Professor of Environmental Engineering in the School of Public Health of the University of North Carolina at Chapel Hill, is indeed a recognized authority on water quality and water safety. In his opinion, "Some 60 to 70 thousand synthetic organic chemicals are already in commerce and others are coming into use at the rate of perhaps 1,000 per year. They are formulated to be long-lasting, and they are not easily degraded."

Of course the United States government sets drinking-water standards that must be observed. As late as 1982, however, only six of these synthetic organics came under government regulation because it was feared that they would contribute to cancer, if ingested over long periods of time. These six are pesticides; the seventh, just added, includes the trihalomethanes. In addition, ten inorganic chemicals also come under government regulation because of their toxic properties. These are arsenic, barium, cadmium, chromium, lead, mercury, selenium, nitrate, silver, and fluoride.

An increasing number of water-quality experts are beginning to view these thousands of new synthetic organic chemicals as "toxic time bombs." Concerning them, Okun says, "Present-day treatment is inadequate. It cannot recognize or sort them all out. So they are discharged into rivers and lakes, injected into the ground, and stored in toxic dumps. Furthermore, their latency period is such that ill health effects may not show up for thirty years or more. And they seldom act alone. They can form into an infinite number of combinations for which testing is clearly impossible."

The whole situation adds up to this: If the water supply is drawn from a polluted source, many of us may come down with diseases in thirty or thirty-five years, diseases for which we haven't even got a name yet.

These are jolting words. But what's the solution?

At the filtration plant in Newburgh, both Goodrich and Haffen can only hope that the day will soon come when scientists will have learned how to handle these organics expeditiously and economically. In the meantime, they advise "the continued careful management of protected upland sources and uncontaminated aquifers— away from industrial and agricultural pollutants."

But to return to that drinking water after it leaves the clear-water well in the Newburgh plant—or for that matter any water-filtration plant. Once water is delivered to the consumer and used, even for the daintiest chores, it is polluted. Drink it, cook with it, wash your floors and clothes with it, flush or shower with it, and this used water becomes waste water. It gurgles down the drain and out of sight. In the United States alone, billions and billions of gallons (1 billion gallons equals 3,785 million liters) of waste water flow through the drains every day. This is sewage—smelly, polluted stuff that no one likes to talk about. People would much rather sing the praises of their waterworks—those gleaming concrete facilities that are backed by sparkling lakes or reservoirs.

But just as the provision for safe drinking water is a municipal responsibility, so too is the control of waste-water pollution a municipal responsibility. Sewage flowing through the drains may be out of sight, but it doesn't just disappear. Ultimately sewage mains lead to a body of water that may actually be the source for the supply of drinking water for the very community that created the waste in the first place. Still, this state of affairs can be corrected. The filthy flowing matter can be and usually is intercepted and diverted to a waste-water treatment facility, which provides primary or secondary treatment.

The primary plant operates on the physical process of sedimentation. It removes the solids in the waste water that would otherwise settle on the bottom of the lake, river, or ocean to which it was discharged. There, those solids would use up the dissolved oxygen in the water.

The secondary plant uses microorganisms that biochemically oxidize the dissolved and colloidal organic material. (Colloidal refers to substances that do not settle out easily and, consequently, use up the dissolved oxygen in the receiving body of water.) This treatment reduces the natural chemicals, bacteria, and viruses. However, it has little effect on synthetic organic chemicals.

Finally, the twice-treated effluent, being relatively clean, is discharged into the nearest body of water.

This would seem to be an ideal way to handle the waste-water problem, but not every community has a waste-water treatment plant. In some instances, even in the United States, there's no such plant at all. In other instances, only primary treatment is provided because money is not available or is diverted to more glamorous projects, such as schools and playgrounds, highways and parks. In still other instances, the plant may break down and spew semitreated waste water into the watercourse, as happened in 1979 at the modern San Jose facility in California. For a month, the secondary filters were clogged. For a month, the waste could be run through only the primary plant. For a month, the San Jose effluent, which empties into San Francisco Bay, was killing off almost all the marine life in the vicinity of the discharge.

Nor is this all there is to the story of waste water. Sometimes, even after secondary treatment, the effluent may still be loaded with harmful levels of nitrogen, phosphorus, heavy metals, and other chemicals. In such instances, tertiary or advanced water treatment is needed, but is not often provided because of the expense.

Clearly, where public drinking water is concerned, public responsibility calls for two kinds of facilities: filtration plants and waste-water treatment plants. Newburgh, as we have seen, manages these facilities, separately and apart from each other. But for an example of comprehensive, integrated management of water, I take you now 3,000 miles (4,828 kilometers) to the west to that shining model in northern California, the Santa Clara Valley Water District. This district is responsible not only for water purification but also for storage, cloud seeding, ground-water recharge, wholesale distribution, and the reclamation of waste water for reuse. In addition, that agency handles all the flood-protection work in area creeks.

In the first of several telephone conversations between this author and James Melton, public information officer of the Santa Clara Valley Water District, Melton asked right off, "Are you writing a book just to tell people how necessary water is and the great benefits it provides? That's my complaint about *water* books. People read them and continue taking water for granted. They think all they have to do is turn on the tap." He paused for breath then continued his attack. "Do you know how incredibly complex our water problems are? Do you know how much it costs to deliver safe water to the public?"

After more phone calls and letters and printed materials, Melton, a caring and dedicated water man, summarized the work of his district: "Almost every drop of rain that falls here goes one of four ways. It can seep into the ground and percolate down to the water basin. It can run into the streams that drain into San Francisco Bay or Monterey Bay. It can evaporate, or it can be used by plants and partly transpired through the leaves. We watch these drops and capture as many as we can. We need them for direct use and for replenishing our ground-water basins."

The most important ground-water basin lies directly beneath the Santa Clara Valley floor and is almost .5 mile (.8 kilometer) in depth. It's like a gigantic bowl filled with sand.

"If you'll consider," said Melton, "that 35 percent of a bowl of water can be poured into a similar-sized bowl of sand without overflowing, you'll get an idea of the tremendous capacity of this particular ground-water basin of ours. However, although this basin is well saturated, it is also well used and needs to be recharged constantly."

"Recharged? How? By precipitation?"

"No. Recharged by us. Otherwise, what happened previously, before this district was organized, might happen again." He was referring to three still-remembered disasters—a dropped water table, land subsidence, and salt intrusion—all related to overpumping.

Land subsidence is a permanent thing. Once the land sinks, it stays that way, no matter how much water may later seep into the ground. That's because underground clay, gravel, and sand particles that had once been separated by water become compacted and can never hold water again. Indeed, according to Melton, "This happened right here where some square miles of the Santa Clara Valley floor dropped as much as 13 feet [4 meters]."

Salt intrusion makes the water unfit to drink. It occurs naturally as excessive withdrawal of fresh water leaves a temporary underground void. Then salt water

Two photographs, one taken in 1914 and the other in 1978, show how much the land has subsided during that period at the South Bay Yacht Club in Aviso, California. (Santa Clara Valley Water District)

moves as it did into some little-used aquifers, near San Francisco.

Since this district operates on integrated manage-

ment, it has developed an enviable number of sources, which include:

• The use of eight dams and eight reservoirs, which capture the rain and the runoff and aid in flood control to some extent. Additionally, the stored water is used throughout the year to replenish the ground-water basin aquifers.

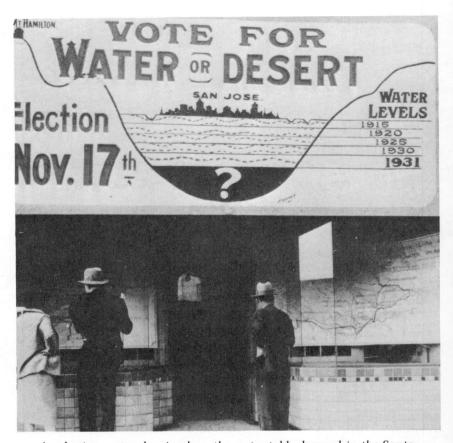

An election poster showing how the water table dropped in the Santa Clara Valley and asking the people to vote for "Water" or "Desert." (Santa Clara Valley Water District)

• The importation of water from the California State Water Project's South Bay Aqueduct, some of which is diverted to recharge, while the rest is filtered through treatment plants for drinking.
• The cloud-seeding activities that have increased rainfall from existing storms by as much as 10 to 15 percent, thus adding thousands of acre feet to the district's water supply.
• The water reclamation program that is providing

what the people of Santa Clara Valley like to call "new" water. This program processes the effluent that's discharged from the sewage treatment plants. The resulting product water is then used for research and for irrigating golf courses and parks, flower and tree nurseries, and selected agricultural and freeway plantings. Some of this water is also used as a barrier against salt-water intrusion in the aquifers.

What is the cost of such a program? According to available reports, the ultimate price of water in the district is kept low by the elected officials, who understand that the key to low cost lies in good management backed by public support. It was public support over the past fifty years that helped float bond issues enabling management to develop its program of expanded storage, treatment, and ground-water recharge, as well as distribution and reclamation facilities.

So much for this model of an integrated system. Add to that their efforts to monitor water usage with an eye to conservation, and the picture becomes nicely rounded.

As James J. Lenihan, director of the Santa Clara Valley Water District, sees it, "We hope that our public information and school education programs will effectively reduce wasteful water-use habits, because this could save more than 10 percent of our supply every year without changing the community's quality of life."

Although the Santa Clara Valley Water District is a model of management, no one yet has come up with the last word in water processing. That is as it should be, because new scientific insights are constantly being developed, while amazing new technologies are constantly being implemented. So we come to Water Factory 21, in Fountain Valley, not far from California's Pacific coastline. This is a water reclamation facility, the newest and largest of its kind in the world, with a capacity of 15 million gallons (56.8 million liters) a day. It starts with

An aerial view of Water Factory 21 located in Fountain Valley, California. (Orange County Water District)

waste water that had received secondary treatment and subjects it to advanced water treatment (AWT) plus reverse osmosis. The result?

"The result," said Information Assistant Lola Handy, when this author called at her Fountain Valley office, "is supplemental water that meets all the requirements of the United States EPA's National Interim Primary Drinking Water Standards. And you know why we call this facility Water Factory 21? Because it's the prototype for the production of such water for the twenty-first century.

"When we went into operation in 1975," Handy went on, "we began processing the effluent from that secondary treatment plant over there, beyond the line of trees. We employ very advanced technology and produce high-quality water that we use for various purposes here, in our Orange County Water District."

"Do these various purposes mean you use this water for drinking?"

Handy laughed. With a mischievous flourish she went to the corner sink, filled a coffeepot, plugged it in, and said, "Come, I'll show you around the plant and let you see the step-by-step reclamation process that—yes—starts with waste-water effluent and produces high-quality water. When we return, you'll know the answer to your question."

The tour of the plant started at the lime-dusted catwalk near the chemical clarification basin. "See," said Handy, "there's the effluent from the secondary treatment plant pouring into the mixing basins. See the lime being stirred in? Oh, yes, we use a lot of lime. For one thing, it hastens flocculation so it quickly clears the water,

A view of the chemical clarification basin at Water Factory 21. (Orange County Water District)

of many suspended solids. And for another, lime starts the process that rids the effluent of its excess nitrogen."

Nitrogen is a no-no to water specialists because it supports the growth of algae and bacteria. But as Handy explained, "A lot of lime mixed in those basins starts a chemical process that goes after the nitrogen by raising the pH."

The term pH, it will be recalled, refers to alkalinity or acidity. A reading of approximately 6 is considered normal, but at "21" ingenious chemists add lime to raise the pH to 11.3, at which level the ammonia ions in the effluent are converted to dissolved ammonia gas. And ammonia is a compound of nitrogen and hydrogen! Once the pH reaches that high level, the effluent is pumped to the top of the ammonia-stripping towers and treated in such a way, with induced air drafts, that the dissolved ammonia gas is released to the atmosphere as the waste water cascades to the bottom.

The specialists then continue with their dual job of bringing the pH down to a normal level and bringing the water quality up to a high level. Accordingly, the effluent is sent along by gravity from the stripping towers to the recarbonation unit, where carbon dioxide gas is bubbled through it, reducing the pH to about 7.5 or 8. Additionally, chlorine is added for algal control.

From the recarbonation unit, the water flows by gravity to and through the multimedia gravity filter—a 30-inch (76.2-meter) bed that is layered with (from top to bottom) coal, silica sand, fine garnet, coarse garnet, and gravel. Here the water is further clarified and now meets turbidity standards.

And still that water—that effluent—moves on, pumped this time to the carbon-adsorption building, where it flows through huge columns, each filled with 43 tons (39 metric tons) of activated granular carbon. Here that water is divested of detergents as well as of some organics that affect color and taste.

Now only two steps remain before the AWT is complete. For the final disinfection, technicians treat the water to a forty-five-minute period in the chlorination tank. And for some further removal of chemicals, minerals, bacteria, viruses, and remaining trace elements that are still lurking in the chlorination tank, the water specialists bring up the heavy artillery. They divert a third of the water from the tank and send it along to the reverse osmosis (RO) unit, which is crowded with tier upon tier of spirally wound, cylindrical filters.

In the RO unit, thundering high-pressure pumps raise the psi (pounds per square inch) from the normal 14.7 at sea level to a monstrous 460. Under such tremendous pressure, the water passing through the RO filters is not only effectively demineralized but also further divested of many minerals, organics, bacteria, viruses, and trace elements. It even comes through with an ideal pH of approximately 6 because of the bit of acid that's automatically added to the feedwater.

Are you wondering why all the water isn't put through the RO unit? It isn't necessary because five parts of RO treated water blended with ten parts of water straight from the chlorination tank is all that's needed to meet the requirements for dissolved solids.

Now the job of Water Factory 21 is done. Now the AWT, which incorporates RO, has reduced the organics found in municipally treated water by 99 percent. Officials at the plant, however, are quick to say that the district continues to conduct extensive research in water quality based on organic identification, virus monitoring, and the effectiveness of the program.

I asked Handy, "What happens to this product water now?"

She replied, "It is again blended—this time with well water, further to dilute the remaining dissolved solids. This blended product is then pumped into the groundwater basin, through twenty-three injection wells. The injected water moves naturally through our four aquifers and serves us in two ways: some halts seawater intrusion, some recharges the basin.''

"Then none of this '21' water is piped directly to the homes for domestic consumption?''

"The answer is, 'No.' What runs out of the kitchen taps is water from the storage reservoir.''

It is to be remembered, however, that the reservoir gets its water from wells sunk into the four aquifers through which trickles that interesting mix of rain that has percolated into the ground, seepage that has moved in from other surface and subsurface sources, and some of the reclaimed water that was injected from Water Factory 21.

"But,'' said Handy as we returned to the office, "we know, on the basis of tests continuously conducted at the reservoir, that the water running out of our taps is far superior to water that's used for drinking in many communities, even in the United States.'' This statement was later confirmed by Dr. James Crook, senior sanitary engineer at California's Department of Health Services.

Somewhat later, over cups of coffee that tasted no different from coffee in other places, Handy's chief, Gordon Elser, reviewed Handy's statements and added, "Our reclaimed water, after it's injected into those twenty-three wells, builds a pressure ridge underground that serves as a barrier against seawater intrusion. It also replenishes our local ground-water supplies and supplements our natural supply, which is limited here in southern California.

"As for the water problems that people fret about—quantity and quality,'' Elser observed, "it's not so much a matter of quantity as availability. And water factories such as ours can substantially increase the availability of water—reclaimed water, it's true, but *supplemental water*, as we choose to call it. However, as you've already heard, it meets all government standards for safety before it's injected into those wells.''

154

"But the cost? Isn't it prohibitive when you consider all the energy used by the pumps and the reverse osmosis unit?"

"For us here, where water is expensive," said Elser, "the cost per gallon [3.78 liters] of reclaimed water is actually competitive with the cost of water that we have to import from other districts or states."

And then he said, "What we're doing here at Factory 21 is managing our water supply in such a way that we make more of it available to our cities and towns."

The Newburgh filtration plant, the integrated program in the Santa Clara Valley, and Water Factory 21 are three examples of sophisticated management of the water supply close to the point of use. These remarkable operations are made possible in the industrialized countries by the availability of money and trained personnel. In the Third World and other countries where money and trained personnel are in short supply, there are other management options, many less expensive and easier to develop. These options start with the *source of the supply* wherever that source might be.

What these options are will be discussed in the next chapter. Also discussed will be ways of developing the sources and delivering the water in accordance with quality needs.

11

More Options for Managing the Fresh-Water Supply

Given contaminated river or lake water, it can be treated at modern waterworks so that it is fit to use, but that process costs good money. Wouldn't it make more sense to clean up the watercourses in the first place and keep them clean? Ask this question at an environmental meeting, and the answer you'd get would be a resounding yes. You'd get the same resounding *yes* from the people who live alongside such watercourses, especially if they'd seen the water running red with the blood and entrails dumped from a slaughter house; or foaming with detergent drained from washing machines; or stinking from the effluent released by a sauerkraut plant or a raw-sewage main.

Mostly it is the sanitary engineers, the public health specialists, and the environmentalists who have been concerned with the deteriorating quality of these watercourses, and it is they who have been proposing some common-sense management options.

Common sense would suggest that one way to make the supply of such water available for our use would be to control the discharge of waste into the rivers and lakes that are tapped for drinking. This can be done and has been done—at times.

The Potomac River is a case in point. The Potomac was an international disgrace in the early 1970s. It was a smelly eyesore that embarrassed American officials whose job it was to entertain foreign dignitaries in Washington, D.C. In its murky waters floated such large clumps of decaying algae—and worse—that swimming was forbidden and fishing impossible since all the fish had died. But after ten years and a billion-dollar cleanup, the Potomac has become a playground for swimmers, boaters, and fishermen, who are likely to catch any of the one hundred species thriving there.

All this came about through the cooperative efforts of the neighboring states. Sewage-treatment plants were upgraded and point-source pollution discharges of industrial and municipal wastes were eliminated. Now the bacterial count is more than satisfactory except after heavy rainstorms when the river swells with debris.

The Ruhr River is another spectacular instance of water cleanup. Once the dirtiest river in Europe, the Ruhr is now the cleanest. Once it carried all the waste from the densely populated, industrialized valley, as well as from the surrounding coal mines; now it abounds with fish and recreational facilities, and it supplies public water at equitable prices.

This improved state of affairs was achieved through determined management that touched the pocketbooks of the river polluters. Industrial enterprises and local authorities were put on notice: they were informed that they would have to pay a levy if their sewage and other wastes were inadequately treated. This was no ordinary levy. It was fixed according to the toxicity of the discharge, and the monies collected were used to finance the construction of new sewage-treatment facilities.

The Germans were able to restore the Ruhr because this river flows entirely within German boundary lines. The Rhine? That's another story because the Rhine is an international river that touches base in five countries—Switzerland, France, Luxembourg, West Germany, and Holland—and it hasn't been easy for these five to develop a cooperative plan for the use of the river. Throughout the years, the water quality has continued to worsen despite an expenditure of some four billion dollars by the West German government in the early 1970s. In fact, a 1978 study found 1,500 chemicals—organic and inorganic—in the water. As a result, a conference was called for the following year to consider the deplorable state of "Father Rhine."

This 1979 conference met in Düsseldorf, and among the delegates attending were water experts, economists, industrialists, landowners, mine owners—and politicians, of course. Here is a partial account of what happened at that conference, as reported by Peter Lewis, Paris correspondent for the New Zealand *Herald:*

"The fishtank was rolled into the conference room on a trolley, and an attendant stepped forward. Under the gaze of the people present, he dropped two goldfish into the brownish water. After darting about in panic for a moment, the fish rose to the surface in an instinctive quest for oxygen, their mouths agape, their tails thrashing.

"A mere fifteen minutes later, they were looking sick. In another two hours, they were floating on their backs, stone dead. The goldfish had succumbed to immersion in a sample of Rhine water."

The goldfish died in the tank, and the people were forbidden to swim in the Rhine—and no wonder, when just the top 6 inches (15 centimeters) of the river were transparent. As one aged delegate pointed out, "Today, only the eels are tough enough to live in that water, but sixty years ago, I used to catch salmon there."

The Düsseldorf conferees gave special attention to the chemical wastes pouring from the West German industrial plants and to the salts draining from the potash mines in Alsace, France. Their recommendations naturally focused on cleanup and control:

• They asked that legislation be enacted to require industrial plants to reveal the chemical breakdown of their effluent because scientists have no way to treat waste water unless they know precisely what chemicals it contains. In addition, it was noted that trying to find out who is dumping what into the Rhine is like looking for a black cat in a dark room.

• They asked that the list of poisons banned from the river be increased from 15 to 150.

• They threatened sanctions against France unless the potash discharges were curbed.

Despite these brave words, no one expected any immediate changes in the management of the Rhine. One and all were of the same opinion: that since the energy crunch, which began in 1973, the European governments have been more interested in keeping the factories running than in keeping the waters and the skies clean.

Cleaning up an international river, be it the Rhine, the Jordan, the Danube, or the Colorado, is understandably a task beset by difficulties because so many political entities are involved. An increasing number of individual countries, however, have been looking into their polluted in-boundary rivers. The very same year that Lewis filed his report with the New Zealand *Herald*, the government of New Zealand sponsored an impressive Water Resources Study of its major river, the Waikato.

This study shows the river running crystalline clear as it leaves Lake Taupo, only to empty into Port Waikato, some 400 miles (644 kilometers) away as a brown, turbid, smelly, unsanitary mess. Along the way, the Waikato serves 33 potable supply systems, 203 irrigation schemes, and 8 hydroelectric power plants. Along the way, too, it is replenished with waste that's discharged from twenty major industrial plants, including twelve dairy factories, two abattoirs, and a large pulp and paper mill. In addition, seeping geothermal waters and uncooled industrial discharges raise the temperature of the river and further the concentration of unwelcome chemicals. These are arsenic, which is hazardous to human health; boron, which adversely affects the growth of crops; and mercury, which enters the food chain and is ultimately absorbed by the very fish that may be served up on New Zealand dinner tables. Nor should the pollutants that trickle into the Waikato from the runoff of the farm fields—fertilizers, pesticides, and animal wastes—be overlooked. These boost the concentration of nitrogen and phosphorus, two nutrients that do the water no good.

This was an effective study that may serve as a model for other countries. It investigated the river system as a whole, collected information, and made it available to the public. Now it's up to management to see about cleaning up the water and ensuring the fair and responsible use of the river. As of the early 1980s, however, such action was still in the planning stage.

Of all the pollutants that pour into the world's rivers and degrade their water quality, none is more ubiquitous and treacherous than silt and its frequent partner, salt. When overloaded with these two contaminants, river water poses serious problems. An excess of salt affects the crops adversely. An excess of silt increases the maintenance and treatment costs. In the past, salty, silty rivers have destroyed great civilizations—even such a one as fabled Babylonia. Within the present century, the salty, silty Colorado has threatened the well-being of one of the most productive agricultural areas ever known—California's irrigated Imperial and Coachella valleys. In the same way, the Salt River has threatened the Phoenix, Arizona, area.

If you've ever traveled through the American Southwest, you've surely seen stretches of dry, white, salt-encrusted farm fields. If you've talked with the farmers, you've surely heard them complain about their salinity problems. For the sake of brevity, let's confine our discussion here to the management of the Colorado. Actually, this water is not so salty that you'd notice if you drank some. It is, however, salty enough to damage plant growth in the irrigated fields unless a favorable salt balance is deliberately maintained.

A favorable salt balance can be maintained only if the input of salt from irrigation water is less than, or no greater than, the output through drainage. If the input is greater, so much salt accumulates in the soil that the field becomes worthless and has to be abandoned.

In southern California, an unfavorable salt balance became noticeable around 1929 as the Colorado became saltier and the practice of irrigation more widespread. So saline irrigation management had to be devised—and it was. With the cooperation of the United States Soil Conservation Service, the Imperial Valley Irrigation Dis-

A deep-drain tiling machine in operation in the Imperial Valley near El Centro, California. (Bureau of Reclamation photo by E. E. Hertzog)

trict has since then installed more than 2,600 miles (4,183 kilometers) of 4-inch (10-centimeter) perforated tile drains in the fields. The tiles are placed at a depth of 6 to 10 feet (2 to 3 meters) or more and spaced anywhere from 50 to 300 feet (15 to 91 meters) apart. They collect the seeped-down irrigation water that percolates through the soil and carries as much as 1.1 tons of salt per acre foot. Then that water runs, by gravity flow, to the drainage ditches that lead to the drainage outlet system. From the drainage outlet system, this water empties into the Salton Sea. Today, more than 400,000 acres are periodically serviced by tile-maintenance crews. And the drainage of that salty irrigation water, plus the leaching water that's used to flush salt away from the surface, is so effective that the valley continues to flourish magnificently.

American farmers, however, weren't the only ones concerned with the river's salinity. In 1961, Mexican farmers began complaining about the sudden sharp increase in the salinity of the Colorado water, which, by international treaty, was being diverted to them at Morelos Dam.

What happened in 1961? The Welton-Mohawk Irrigation and Drainage District began pumping its salt-laden drainage water into the Colorado River!

Almost twenty years were to pass before the excessive salinity of the river could be corrected. The Americans built two bypass drainage systems, routed the district's salty drainage away from the Colorado, carried it all the way to the Santa Clara Slough, and so satisfied the legal claims of Mexico.

Such are the problems that a salty river poses to technology, and such are the headaches it delivers to the people who use it. Bypass drains got high priority, as did concrete-lined irrigation canals, but because the salty water continued to flow into the drainage outlet systems, the headaches continued. Too much water was being lost out to that Santa Clara Slough, so there were more talks and more discussions among engineers, water experts, and farmers until the thinking began to center around another kind of bypass: a desalting plant.

In due time the Colorado River Basin Salinity Project was evolved. Under this plan, the drainage water from the irrigation district would be channeled through a desalination facility near Yuma, Arizona. There the water would be demineralized by reverse osmosis and then, minus much of its salt, would be returned to the Colorado River. However, this didn't happen overnight. Not until 1978 were contracts awarded for the construction of this plant. Not until 1979 was ground broken so construction could get under way. Not until 1986 is the plant scheduled to begin operation with a capability of desalting 73.1

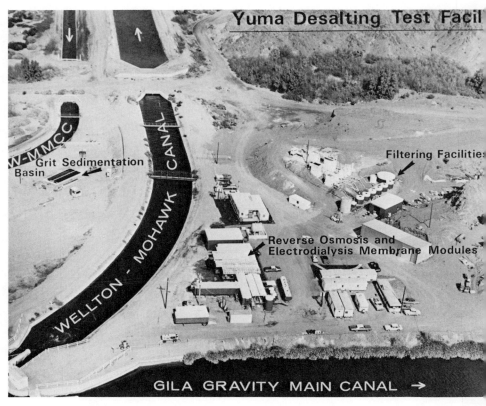

An aerial view of the Yuma Desalting Test Facility. (Bureau of Reclamation photo by E. E. Hertzog)

million gallons (276.7 million liters) per day of irrigation return flows. At that point, the desalted water will be entirely acceptable for delivery to Mexico and the bypass to the slough will go out of operation.

Let's not, however, forget that other problem—silt. Although the Colorado had run silty for decades, people used to joke about it and say, "That water? It's too thick to drink and too thin to plow." However, as agriculture expanded, muddy water was no longer a joke. Yet, creative engineers solved this problem spectacularly in the 1930s.

At that time the Bureau of Reclamation was constructing the Imperial Dam, which was to divert Colorado water into the new All-American Canal.

"We'll have to do something about the silt in that water," said the engineers. And the farmers said, "Yes. When that muddy water starts flowing through the canal and its subsidiaries, the irrigation ditches will silt up."

The old method of managing silting-up problems was to shovel and dredge. But the ingenious engineers working on this project thought up a better way. They devised the idea of *desilting basins* for the Imperial Dam, and it was a first in the world of irrigation.

To find out what desilting basins are and how they operate, this author went to see Bill Montana, assistant superintendent of the Imperial Irrigation District at Imperial Dam. Montana, a tall, loping fellow, is an enthusiastic water expert whose career started by chance while he was still in high school. As he tells it, he had been assigned to do a paper on Colorado River silt and thought to himself, "How boring. What's to know about silt? But here I am now," he said, as we toured the area in his air-conditioned pick-up, "working on the most exciting river pollutant there is and controlling it." He parked the truck

A view of one of the All-American Canal desilting basins at Imperial Dam showing the rotating scraper mechanisms. (Bureau of Reclamation photo by E. E. Hertzog)

on the road overlooking the basins and said with considerable pride, "Would you believe that more than sixty nations with desilting problems have sent their engineers here to find out how our basins work?"

The six basins, each 14 feet (4.3 meters) deep, look calm and peaceful, like proverbial millponds, but they're not. That's because the muddy Colorado water, diverted by the dam, races in at a rate of 7 cubic feet (2 cubic meters) per second. Here, as the velocity is abruptly checked, much of the silt drops to the bottom. To prevent a buildup of that mud, the basins have been equipped with huge clarifiers with rotating scrapers. Each scraper makes a complete revolution every thirteen minutes and, while doing so, churns up the mud, which the clarifiers suck in and swallow. (See the photograph on page 165.)

You wonder what happens to that mud? It flows through underground pipes back to the Colorado River, below Imperial Dam. The sediment is then sluiced to a *settling basin* two miles downstream, and there it quietly sinks to the bottom. After that, a dredge periodically pumps the silt from the floor of that settling basin and scatters it about the surrounding low-lying flood plain. Meanwhile, back at the desilting basins, the clear water is skimmed from the top and directed to the All-American Canal, which is 80 miles (129 kilometers) long and 21 feet (6.4 meters) deep.

Today, clear Colorado water irrigates southern California by way of the All-American Canal and its 3,000-mile (4,828-meter) network of branching canals and laterals. Not only is the quality of this water well managed; so is its delivery to farmers. Orders for water are placed by computer, and the water arrives at the fields at the time it's supposed to be there.

Beauforth Bradley, Water Master of the Imperial Irrigation District, handles these orders. Bradley, a man of vast experience, works out of the district headquarters, where he is flanked by a staff of lab technicians, chemists, and three kinds of engineers (hydraulic, civil, and mechanical) who spend most of their time checking field conditions. In his office, Bradley is eager to show visitors his evaporation pans, ledgers of accounts and billings to farmers for water received ("because they have to pay for the water, you know—$7.50 an acre foot"), and his stacks of maps. His pride and joy is the huge wall map labeled WATER TRANSPORTATION—HOOVER DAM TO USER, which is animated. It shows a simulated blue Colorado River flowing from Hoover Dam to Imperial Dam, into the All-American Canal. (See the map on pages 168-169.) But it's the banks of meters with their flickering colored lights that are basic to the operation of this office because those meters show, among other things, wind speed and direction—two factors that affect the time flow of the Colorado.

Because the water that's needed to irrigate this district must come from far-off Lake Mead (Hoover Dam), Bradley needs to place the water orders well in advance. As he receives these orders from the individual landowners, he collates them and sends them along to the office at Imperial Dam. From there, the district order goes to Hoover Dam, and the amazing transportation schedule begins. If you follow the notations on the Water Transportation map, you will see how the landowners can count on getting their water when they want it. If, as in this instance, they want it delivered between April 14 and 20, the water is released from Hoover Dam on April 13 to start on its 146-hour journey. Down the Colorado it flows, down to Imperial Dam, down to the All-American Canal, down to the last fields at the Vail lateral, at the end of which the irrigation gates are closed.

The wise management of rivers as a way to augment the supply of fresh water is surely the first common-sense option. However, even if it were possible to maintain the world's rivers in superlative condition, there'd still be a shortage of high-quality water.

Why? Because in most cities, as well as in some rural areas, the high-quality water is delivered to consumers as

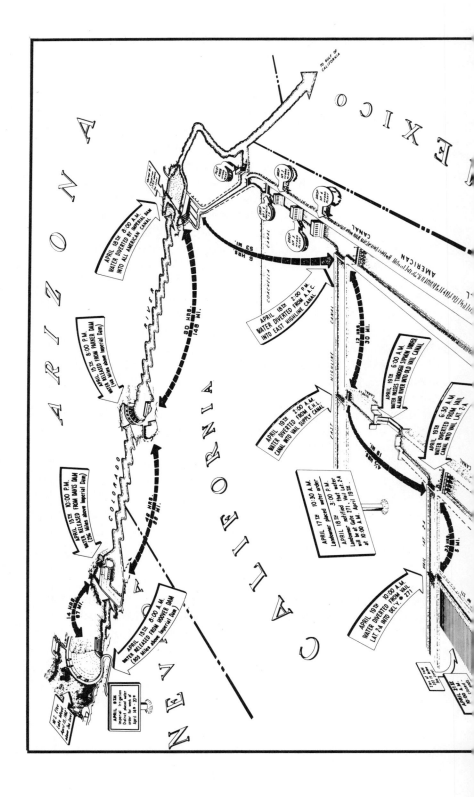

IMPERIAL IRRIGATION DISTRICT

WATER TRANSPORTATION

HOOVER DAM TO USER

Water transportation from Hoover Dam to the user, showing the time-table needed for an on-time delivery. (Imperial Irrigation District, Imperial, California) all-purpose water. Of course, high-quality water is essential to our health, but is it essential to the health of a toilet bowl that needs flushing? Or a sidewalk that needs hosing? Or a car that needs washing? It's clear that there is a *hierarchy of water needs.* That being so, it makes sense to consider a *hierarchy of water-quality alternatives.*

The idea of quality alternatives is not new. The ancient Romans not only considered water quality alternatives, but they actually set up *dual supply systems.* Some of their aqueducts delivered seawater for cleaning jobs. Other aqueducts delivered sweet mountain-spring water for drinking and cooking. Ocean liners and war vessels have long used dual water systems on shipboard. And today, the City of Hong Kong uses a dual system—importing water for drinking, but piping in seawater for nonpotable uses.

If only it were feasible to develop dual water systems for every city and town. One system would carry only potable supplies from high-quality upland sources for the people. The other would carry nonpotable supplies for all the jobs that use up to 90 percent of the total water requirements in any given area. Now since the nonpotable water would be drawn from polluted surface sources and from partially reclaimed waste water, it might be somewhat discolored, brackish, or even smelly, but with twentieth-century technology, the water specialists would see that it was sanitized, clarified, odor-free, bacteriologically safe, and not a health hazard when used as intended, for nonpotable purposes.

The reclamation of waste water from sewers and industrial discharges and its subsequent reuse for nonpotable purposes is increasing in many countries. This is not only sound water management; it is also good business, as you can see by the illustration on page 172.

Reclaiming waste water is such good business that more than five hundred American localities are operating such projects and selling the water at scaled-down prices

The cooling towers in Burbank, California, where the Public Works Department uses 2 million gallons (7.5704 million liters) a day of disinfected high-quality secondary effluent for cooling. (Daniel A. Okun, from Guidelines for Water Reuse, *Camp Dresser & McKee, Inc., Boston, Mass., 1980)*

for agricultural and landscape irrigation, industrial cooling, ground-water recharge, fish propagation, and more. These projects are scattered over some two dozen states in such places as Burbank, California; the Naval Base at Norfolk, Virginia; and Westminster, Colorado. And everywhere, no one loses when a dual water-supply system is implemented.

Groundwater Recharge	Recreational/ Environmental	Agricultural	Nonpotable Urban	Industrial
Water-table management Development of salt water intrusion barrier	Lakes and ponds Marsh enhancement Streamflow enhancement Fisheries Snowmaking	Crop irrigation Commercial nurseries Commercial aquaculture	Landscape irrigation Fire protection Air-conditing Toilet-flushing	Cooling Boiler-feed Process Water Construction uses

(Reprinted from Consulting Engineer, *September 1979, Volume 53, No. 3, pp. 96–103, Copyright by Technical Publishing, a company of the Dun & Bradstreet Corporation, 1982—all rights reserved.)*

However, older cities would find it very expensive to unhook from their present all-purpose water systems and install a nonpotable system alongside it. Imagine the cost and the field day the plumbing contractors would have. Still, it's not an impossible task, as the people of St. Petersburg, Florida, have shown. This city has just recently "retrofitted" its distribution system and now operates an excellent dual supply arrangement.

It's in the new cities, newly constructed on large tracts of unused land, that dual water systems are often put in. And just as new cities can readily manage dual installations, so too can the newly developing countries.

Desert-bound Kuwait is one such developing country with a dual supply system. Their engineers desalt seawater in modern distillation plants that run on low-cost electricity generated at oil-fired power stations. They then blend the distilled product with some of their limited ground-water reserve to improve the taste. After that, they store it in reservoirs and elevated cone-shaped towers. This is Kuwait's potable supply, ready to be piped to towns and rural water-filling stations. For their nonpotable needs, Kuwaitis tap their brackish aquifers. Pumping crews raise the undrinkable water and store it in separate reservoirs and towers. Technicians turn the distribution valves, and off that water flows through its own pipe network, which runs parallel to the fresh-water network. In a somewhat similar manner, the people of Saudi Arabia are also served by a dual water-supply system.

As you see, there really are common-sense options for managing the world's fresh-water supply so that it goes further. Processing waste water, controlling river and lake pollution, and installing dual supply systems are just three of these options. "But there's still another solution to the erratic shortages of potable water, and that is *water management on a regional scale.*" This is the opinion of Daniel Okun, who spent his 1974 sabbatical year in England and Wales studying their regionalization of water management.

In planning a regionalization program, engineers study the terrain as they check out the many small water systems, each draining its own small watershed. The many small watersheds make up a large one, usually called a regional drainage basin. It's these drainage basins that interest the engineers, the water authorities, the community planners, and the economists. They regroup all the small systems within a region into one large system and place a single Water Authority (WA) in charge of the entire works.

Okun was in England and Wales when their 1,609 various-sized water and waste-water systems, serving some 50 million people, were regrouped into ten regional systems. "This was no paper regrouping," says Okun, "because each water authority was given responsibility (save for minor exceptions) for the ownership, planning, design, construction, operation, and finance of the facilities."

Responsibility often means only what people want it

to mean, and that's why some projects fail while others succeed. In this instance, success was assured under a responsibility umbrella that mandated:

- the conservation, augmentation, distribution, and use of water resources and the provision of water supplies;
- the collection of sewage, the treatment of sewage and waste water, and the provision for the disposal of the effluent;
- the restoration and maintenance of the wholesomeness of rivers and inland waters, as well as estuaries and coastal waters;
- the use of inland waters for recreation and the enhancement of amenity values of these waters;
- land drainage and the prevention of flooding; and
- fisheries and navigation in inland waters.

So it came to pass that in England and Wales, regionalization of water management has been a great success, as you can see by the record of accomplishment of the ten water authorities. They were even able to manage the 1976 drought, which was the worst in history, and to maintain services with little fluster or confusion. How? By transferring large volumes of high-quality water from one watershed to another in any given region. They were, additionally, able to show significant economies of scale. They found it was cheaper to build and operate a large plant rather than several smaller ones. They also found that further economies were made possible by judicious siting of treatment facilities. All in all, they will tell you, it is easier and cheaper to provide effective surveillance of ten large systems than of 1,609 various-sized ones.

At this point, we need to pause and think again about the world's escalating demand for potable water. Although countless scientists are searching for new sources of fresh water, others are devising new ways to control pollution, and still others are inventing ingenious ways to process and reclaim waste water, the fact remains that such operations are all very costly.

For the world to make the best use of its finite supply of fresh water, there's really only one solution: to make every drop count.

12

Making Every Drop Count— Technologically

Although the demand for low-cost, high-quality water is becoming acute, it will undoubtedly become less acute in time. Good management, plus sophisticated technology and the continued development of nonconventional sources, will assure the supply. However, we will probably continue to hear cries of shortage and woe unless the *utilization* of the supply is equally well managed.

Only a comprehensive water policy will make it possible for each sector of the economy—domestic, industrial, and agricultural—to get its equitable share at a fair price. As it is, the users are staging water wars. Here in the United States, for example:

• Farmers in thriving irrigation districts are competing with the residents of new high-rise buildings for the local water supply.

• States using a common river are trying to capture as much water as they can for themselves, engaging in judicial battles and challenging court decisions.

• Other states are trying to break old Indian agreements.

Nor are the courts very helpful in adjudicating claims because what water legislation there is happens to be quite chaotic. This is a situation that dates back to 1783, when the Revolutionary War ended and each of the colonies became a sovereign state with all the rights and responsibilities formerly held by the English King and Parliament. Old Spanish land grants further complicate the water laws in the West and Southwest. To this day, almost all governmental powers concerning water reside with the individual states, and each state writes its own laws concerning water ownership and use. Some are common laws, which are judge-made, and others are statutory laws, which are the product of legislative bodies. Note, however, that these laws are not based on water science. Does the Colorado River confine itself legally to the state of Colorado? Do the snows on the Oregon mountains melt

177

and run off only into Oregon reservoirs? No, some of that meltwater runs off to the rivers, and some seeps into the ground and percolates through the aquifers. And aquifers, you will recall, run every which way in terms of the geologic structure, so who knows where they deliver their water? To a local well? To the next state? To a city a thousand miles away? And who owns the water moving in those aquifers? Who has the right to impound it? Divert it?

As the the King says in the play *Anna and the King of Siam*, " 'Tis a puzzlement." In real life, though, it's only when the puzzlement begins to hurt that people turn from talk to action. That's exactly what happened in 1959, when the Israeli government adopted a national water policy, which, by *making every drop count*, turned that semiarid country into a model of agricultural and industrial productivity.

According to this law, "The water resources of the State of Israel are public property, under state control, and intended for the needs of its residents and the development of the country." Since there is no private ownership of water, a person must obtain a license for tapping or developing any source of water, even on his own property. In addition, the amount of water he may produce, withdraw, or use is allocated by the Water Commission.

People accustomed to laissez faire—to doing their own thing—are not likely to favor such a strong national policy or such a powerful water commission. But as we approach the twenty-first century, it's becoming quite clear that our concept of water management has been incomplete. Although many states are doing a fairly good job of developing and delivering potable water supplies, they are not doing much of a job of managing the utilization of those supplies effectively. In many sectors more water is wasted than is actually used.

Here is how water is generally utilized in the United States after it's received by the consumers:

  • In the domestic sector, we see water pouring from

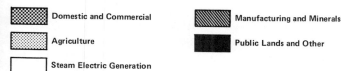

CONSUMPTION

- ▨ Domestic and Commercial
- ▨ Manufacturing and Minerals
- ▦ Agriculture
- ■ Public Lands and Other
- ☐ Steam Electric Generation

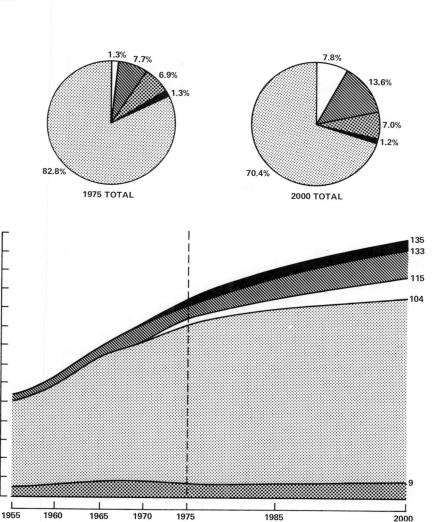

1975 TOTAL

1.3% 7.7%
6.9%
1.3%
82.8%

2000 TOTAL

7.8%
13.6%
7.0%
1.2%
70.4%

Billion gallons per day

135
133
115
104

9

1955 1960 1965 1970 1975 1985 2000

Consumption, by functional use

A graph showing water use in the United States. (U.S. Water Resources Council)

the hydrants, leaking from the pipes, and dripping from the faucets. We hear the media urging us to conserve—which some do and most don't. Yet, there are ways to make people conserve. Metering will do it every time—metering in every apartment, office, social center, school, and shop—plus a sliding scale of charges: so much for the first 100 gallons (378.5 liters) used, so much more for the second hundred, and so on. The more a private person uses, the more costly his water becomes.

But remember that domestic and commercial water accounts for only 6.9 percent of the total water use in this country. Suppose metering and sliding charges were to cut that down to 3.9 percent. Would that silence the cries of shortage and woe? Not likely, unless the industrial and agricultural sectors become responsible for their share. Otherwise, they would just tap the remaining 96 percent of the supply with their same old inefficient utilization practices.

• Industry is the next largest user of water because it requires large quantities for steam, electrical generation, manufacturing, and mining. It also needs cooling water to condense steam into liquid water and to protect machinery from excessive heat; feedwater for the boilers when they're fired up to make steam; and water for processing during manufacture, or when something is being dissolved or cooked or canned. Finally, industry needs water to dispose of its waste.

But excessive dumping of waste into rivers and lakes has degraded the quality of the water. When the local supply gets overloaded with salts, industrialists face corrosion and scaling problems. When it gets overloaded with nitrate, copper, or iron, the beer brewers have to either go in for costly water treatment or go out of business.

In many instances, the water that industry requires must be high quality, the kind that meets the standards of the Environmental Protection Agency. For some chemical

processes, it must be absolutely pure. For most other purposes, however, reclaimed water is acceptable.

With the increasing use of reclamation, as well as
recycling within factories, industry's utilization of water
is becoming ever more efficient, but it has a long way to go
before it can score an A.

• It's in the agricultural sector that we find the nation's biggest water customers, and it is they who account
for almost 83 percent of the nation's total fresh-water use.
Because the world needs ever more food, farmers will
need ever more water every year.

Still, despite water shortages in some areas, the number of irrigated farm acres has risen sharply: from 37
million in 1958, to 44 million in 1967, to 58 million in
1977. (An acre equals .4 hectare.) A recent study shows
that the rate of change to irrigation has accelerated to 1.4
million acres (.56 million hectares) a year during the last
decade. Why? Because irrigation water is cheap in areas
that are subsidized by the federal government, as in the
Imperial Valley. There the price is $7.50 per acre foot
(1,233 cubic meters). In nearby Los Angeles, however,
residents must pay $225 an acre foot. Understandably,
hard feelings are rife. City folks, when they think about
it, claim their tax dollars are supporting the subsidy.
Farmers claim they can stay in business and keep food
prices low only if the water rates are low. Government
officials say irrigation water costs less because it is generally of poorer quality and delivered to the farms by gravity, whereas city water must be filtered and chlorinated
and pumped to each residence, shop, school, store—
whatever.

Subsidized water is a great boon to farmers, but it is
not likely to motivate them to use their supply efficiently.
As a matter of fact, the Soil Conservation Service of the
Department of Agriculture published a report in 1980,
America's Soil and Water: Conditions and Trends, that's
rather startling. It shows irrigation water being wasted so

casually that inefficiency seems to be built in. Of the great volume of water, 158.7 billion gallons (600.7 billion liters), diverted *each day* for irrigation use from streams and lakes and reservoirs during a "normalized" year, only 65.7 billion gallons (248.7 billion liters), or 41 percent, was consumed by the crops, most of it moving later to the atmosphere through evapotranspiration. But 93.1 billion gallons (352.4 billion liters), or 58 percent, was lost or spilled, either during delivery to the farms or after it got there. Of this lost or spilled water, 72.3 billion gallons (273.7 billion liters) was returned to the source. About 20.8 billion gallons (78.7 billion liters) was neither returned nor used by the crops.

Clearly, the conveyance systems are at fault in that they carry more water than they deliver. Conveyance systems for irrigation water average 78 percent efficiency, and on-farm irrigation systems average only 53 percent efficiency. According to the report, "Today's practices leave much room for improvement, both in regulating the timing and the amount of water delivered to the plants, and in preventing water loss during delivery."

All this is true, but a visitor touring the fields in the American Southwest, as this author did in the fall of the year, can only be favorably impressed by what he or she sees.

Looking at mile upon mile of Imperial Valley farmland planted in broccoli, cantaloupe, carrots, garlic, lettuce, cucumbers, and squash, you might imagine that the irrigation water flowing in the laterals comes from an inexhaustible planetary fountain. This impression is reinforced by the thousands of bales of harvested alfalfa stacked tier upon tier along the roadsides. All the irrigation systems are most impressive.

In some sections, you can see level, or dead-basin, irrigation. This is a gravity-flow method whereby the water is flooded over a field for a short period. The water stays there until it's absorbed, but to ensure even absorption, the field must be properly prepared. It must be leveled to about 1-inch (2.5-centimeter) tolerance for water control. If you're lucky, you will see a laser land-leveling machine working a field. You'll see the operator riding in the high cab of the tractor that's picking up the beam from the parked transmitter unit. And you'll see him watching carefully the adjustment of the scrapers that are dragging behind the tractor. You're doubly lucky if you

A laser-beam sending unit and a tractor pulling a scraper equipped with a receiving unit that automatically controls the land-leveling process. (Bureau of Reclamation photo by C. W. Siegel)

are there early enough and find Arthur Kuhn on the field supervising the work between plantings.

Kuhn, a well-muscled, sun-tanned outdoor man, heads Farmers Land-Leveling, Inc., which has eight laser transmitter units and sixteen tractor-scraper machines, each equipped with laser receiving units. Easy to talk to, he leans against the shady side of his pickup truck and recalls the old days. "Then they used horses to draw crude scrapers across the fields. Now, with our fast machines, we move 15 cubic yards (11.5 cubic meters) of earth at a time. We scrape it from the high spots and spread it into the low spots—all by instructions from the laser transmitter."

"Is it necessary to be so technical—to scrape a field to a precise 1-inch [2.5-centimeter] tolerance?" I asked.

"Yes. And for high-value crops, we set the scrapers to .1-inch [.254-centimeter] tolerance. Actually, farming will become even more technical," he said. "Unless a field is really level, with no ups and downs, you'll get irrigation water draining into the little hollows. This will cause salt to accumulate. And excess salt and water will rot those little seedlings. The way labor and energy costs are these days, farmers need 100 percent return on everything they plant. Besides, a laser-leveled field is ideal for leaching purposes—for getting the salt to drain into the ground."

Although level-basin irrigation (also called flood irrigation) has been used since ancient times in Russia, Egypt, Persia, China, and Italy, laser-leveling is the latest thing in high technology. "And," said Kuhn, "its use is expanding. Here in the Southwest, I get more calls for my machines every year."

The impression that America's irrigation systems are topnotch (and they are) is strengthened as one travels through the Southwest. In addition to level-basin irrigation, you can see endless fields that are furrowed to receive the water flowing from the laterals by gravity. This is called furrow irrigation, an ancient practice that farm-

A farmer irrigates his safflower crop on a furrowed field in the Salt River Project, Arizona. (Bureau of Reclamation)

A permanent sprinkler system serves a citrus grove in Florida. (USDA—Soil Conservation Service photo by O. S. Polston)

ers like well enough because even the poorest can afford it. However, it can be wasteful of water because so much seeps into the ground and evaporates into the air. "Still," as one farmer pointed out, "some of my water that's seeped into this field shows up downslope on my other field."

You can also see fields that are too rough, too shallow, or too porous to be effective for flooding or furrowing. Such fields are well served by the sprinkler systems. Although sprinklers are more expensive because they call for more pumps and pipes, energy and labor, farmers find they get a good return on their plantings of row crops and grain, as well as of pasture grass for grazing animals. They also find that they can premix fertilizer into the water before it's applied to the fields.

You may even see occasional fields under drip irrigation by which perforated plastic pipes release filtered water containing dissolved fertilizer directly to each of the plants. The concept of applying water directly to each plant has a long history of utilization in greenhouse culture, but its use for farm crops was not practical till low-cost plastic tubing became available after the early 1960s. The first field application of drip irrigation actually came about by accident! It seems that an observant researcher had happened to notice that a tree growing near a leaking faucet exhibited more vigorous growth than the other trees in the area, which were being irrigated by conventional means. So the idea to extend "dripping" to individual plants was born.

Drip irrigation was introduced in California in 1970, in an avocado grove that covered some 12,000 acres (4,800 hectares). Now these groves were located in San Diego County, where the price of water was high and the hills were steep. Obviously, adaptive research was badly needed, so the University of California Cooperative Extension set up a five-year experiment to compare the two irrigation systems: sprinkler and drip. They set aside a 5-acre (2-hectare) test orchard of 647 trees and served half with sprinklers, the other half with drip. Their 1976 report showed a number of pluses for the drip method: successful growth on those steep hillsides, reduced use of water, and reduced soil salinity.

Drip irrigation has opened marginal lands to agricultural production in arid zones of the world where the climate is favorable for intensive crop production. Thus, drip systems will continue to expand in those areas where every drop of water counts.

All in all, we have here splendid irrigation systems, but all of them, except for the drip system, are wasteful of

A young citrus orchard under drip irrigation in California. A worker is holding one of the drip outlets located at each tree. (USDA—Soil Conservation Service photo by Linden Brooks)

A traveling trickle irrigation system on a cotton field near Tucson, Arizona. (USDA—ARS, Western Region, Water Management Research Laboratory, photo by Michael Sikorski)

water. As that 1980 report indicated, this wastefulness accounts for the agricultural sector calling for 83 percent of the nation's total water use but utilizing only 41 percent of it.

Far to the east, semiarid Israel gets high marks for irrigation efficiency because it utilizes 70 to 80 percent of the water that flows from the source. It has decreased the water input per dunan by 20 percent (4 dunans equal 1 acre or approximately .4 hectare) and has increased the value of its agricultural returns by 100 percent in terms of constant prices. This is how it is done.

Some of Israel's irrigation systems are managed by an automated minicomputer. Field sensors provide the computer with a rundown on the ever changing conditions of each cultivated area of fruit, vegetable, and horticultural crops. For pressure irrigation systems, the computer processes the data and releases to the sprinklers the exact amount of water that the field should get. When the water is gone, the sprinklers shut themselves off.

In the same way, the computer controls the amount of water that's delivered by trickle irrigation (the Israeli term for drip irrigation). This system is portable in that the long perforated plastic pipes are laid out in the fields by machine when and where they are needed.

This author, wondering how tricklers compared with sprinklers in the matter of efficiency, telephoned Jacob Avni, agricultural counselor at the Israeli Embassy in Washington, D.C.

"Well," said Avni, "in regions where we use *brackish water* and where the soil is not the best—neither very fertile nor very good at holding moisture—in those regions and under those conditions, tricklers give better results than sprinklers. We've had comparative success in raising vegetable crops—tomatoes, strawberries, eggplants, and artichokes, also grapes and flowers and more—in the open fields, under plastic covers, and in greenhouses. But, I would say that the results in our orchards with citrus and avocados are, as yet, less promising."

Asked about the consumption of water, Avni said, "With tricklers we save water because there's no chance for the drops to evaporate or fly away with the wind."

Returning to the subject of brackish water, Avni explained that it is only relatively saline. "When those waterdrops fall from the trickler, the salt concentrates on the ground in a whitish pattern you can easily see. And since the water content in the root zone is kept high with this system, the salt concentration there remains low and the plant thrives. But note," he added, "that this kind of water would never do for sprinkle irrigation because the salt would cause leaf burn on the sensitive crops. With the tricklers, we just have to watch soil salinity. If the winter rains don't do a good job of leaching, then the fields are flooded in the spring to finish the job."

But how does that system work? How does it manage to deliver water where and when it's wanted? Israel has an integrated system that's tied in with the country's "water grid," of which the major component is the National Water Carrier. This is a transport system composed of tunnels, pipes, pumping stations, and cement-lined canals that bring the surplus water from the Sea of Galilee, in the north, to the dry agricultural areas in the center and south. Other components of the grid consist of all the other water projects and facilities. The whole system is directed by the Water Commission, which oversees the development and use of all the water sources. It determines allocations, and it establishes an equitable pricing system based on metering and on the efficiency with which the water is utilized. In short, the commission zealously upholds the 1959 Water Law that proclaimed water to be a public property under state control.

And yet, and yet, and yet . . . despite the Water Commission's tight control over every drop allocated to agriculture, despite its drive to reduce unnecessary use of water in the homes, and despite its insistence that industry upgrade its processes and recycle its water, the country continues to need more water. That's because it is using more than 90 percent of its *total ground water and surface supply every year.* Under such conditions, there is no room for further growth in business or agriculture until new, nonconventional water sources are developed and proven to be economically sound.

This is a situation that may well catch up with other agro-industrial nations. These nations may find that with all their technological expertise and conservation drives, they, too, don't have a dependable surplus of usable water at affordable prices. Besides the development of nonconventional sources, such as desalination and cloud-seeding, they will then want to encourage those farsighted research scientists who are moving on another front.

This front is propelled by botanists, biologists, and specialists in desert agriculture as they work in their laboratories, test plots, and fields. These men and women are searching for plants that require very little fresh water, yet grow well and produce acceptable yields. Accordingly, they are exploring distant regions for little-known strains that can get along without much water, and they are hybridizing, that is, developing new strains or varieties through cross pollination.

What exciting scientific ventures we have here! And they may turn out to be very significant ventures. They promise to extend the cultivation of food and fiber crops to marginal lands by natural means, *without the use of expensive water conversion technologies.*

13

Making Every Drop Count— Biologically

The development of new plant varieties is not a new idea. As Thomas Jefferson, third president of the United States, so wisely observed, "The greatest service that can be rendered to any country is to add a useful plant to its culture." So, while hydrogeologists, engineers, and water scientists are working like technological beavers to increase the availability of fresh water, botanists, plant biologists, geneticists, and agronomists (specialists in scientific soil management and field crop production) are working like magicians to *decrease* the amount of fresh water that plants need.

Of course, science isn't magic, but some botanists, biologists, and agronomists are producing three-way results that look like magic. They are doing this with new cultivars—new varieties of food plants—that don't call for much fresh water. Of course, this work is still in the developmental stage, and in most instances the plants are in no way ready for commercial propagation. Nevertheless, the results are promising.

- Some of these plants are *salt tolerant*. Because they can thrive under saline conditions, their cultivation may, in time, be extended to salt marshes, estuaries, and intertidal zones, as well as hitherto unused semiarid regions where the soil is heavily salted.
- Some are *drought resistant*, enabling them to thrive with a minimum amount of rain or irrigation.
- Some are bred to dwarf size, which makes it possible for an acre of them to thrive on less water than an acre of similar but full-sized plants.

American plant biologists began searching for such plants quite a few decades ago. Because this country is flanked by the salty sea on two sides and plagued, to a certain extent, by saline water in some rivers and by saline soil on some farmlands, the scientists turned their attention to food plants that might be *naturally* salt tolerant. They found, for example, that spinach and asparagus are quite salt tolerant, tomatoes and cucumbers are moderately salt tolerant, but green beans are so sensitive that they can tolerate only a minimum of salt. See the chart below.

The salt tolerance of vegetable crops

Tolerant	Moderately tolerant	Sensitive
Garden beets	Tomatoes	Radishes
Kale	Broccoli	Celery
Asparagus	Cabbage	Green beans
Spinach	Cauliflower	
	Lettuce	
	Sweet corn	
	Potatoes (White Rose)	
	Sweet potatoes and yams	
	Bell peppers	
	Carrots	
	Onions	
	Peas	
	Squash	
	Cucumbers	

(Agricultural Research Service, USDA)

With this information, some farmers have been able to irrigate certain of their vegetable crops with water right out of a salty river instead of having to import fresh.

Many scientists, however, are extraordinarily curious and creative and cannot rest unless they are experimenting with something. And so they wonder what if they used a "biological fix" and adapted an economically useful land plant to a saline environment? What if, by careful selection and crossbreeding, they developed a variety that not only was salt tolerant but also retained the desirable characteristics of the land plant?

By the 1970s, a few jubilant researchers were reporting success. Chief among them were Dr. Emanuel Epstein and his graduate student Jack Norlyn, of the University of California at Davis. They selected strains of barley known to be relatively salt tolerant. They grew these strains on a ridge of sand dunes, irrigated with Pacific Ocean water and dilutions of it, and at harvest time had yields that were most gratifying.

Epstein and Norlyn did more—lots more—but they are particularly pleased with their hybridized tomatoes. They planted the seeds of a small, bitter, inedible, salt-tolerant tomato that grows wild along the coast of the Galapagos Islands of Ecuador. They crossbred it with a domestic line. What they got after additional breeding was progeny that bore good-sized delicious tomatoes while growing bravely in a 70 percent solution of seawater!

Research in the development of salt-tolerant strains of cotton as well as wheat and other grains is also continuing, but not just because scientists are curious. It's because cotton is a major fiber, and the grains serve as the food staple for most of the world, especially people in the developing countries. As it is, the people in those countries rarely get enough grain to eat because they cannot raise enough, and they cannot raise enough because their access to fresh-water sources is severely limited.

Epstein believes that "up until now, the problems of saline soils and saline waters were dealt with almost exclusively by manipulating the mineral substrate, by reclamation and drainage as in the Imperial Valley. [Substrate refers to the soil and the water in it.] Now, with the increasing need for usable water and energy, there is a major reason for pursuing as well the novel strategy of selecting and breeding salt-tolerant crops. We have shown that seawater irrigation is possible, given suitable conditions. We feel therefore that this kind of research can, and should, be extended to rangeland and forage crops as well as to human food."

Other researchers in other countries seem to agree. And work continues as they select and try to hybridize ever better salt-tolerant strains of various plants, particu-

195

larly cotton and corn, wheat, sorghum, and rice. Yes, the salt-tolerant plants are coming!

The drought-resistant plants are also coming. On the deserts nature supports many such plants, but one that is of special interest to the International Center for Arid and Semiarid Land Studies in Lubbock, Texas, is the Four-Wing saltbush *(Atriplex canescens)*. This saltbush thrives in dry and saline regions throughout western North America. It is an excellent feed for domestic animals and wildlife even in winter when all the grasses are dormant. It transplants readily to disturbed or overgrazed sites where water is in short supply and is consequently of great interest to cattle ranchers. Researchers at the center believe that the saltbush has the potential of becoming a major world crop for animal feed.

For the farm fields, however, plant biologists have to invent their own drought-resistant strains. They do this by developing new improved hybrids with the kind of survival characteristics that distinguish the desert plants.

Dr. Milton A. Sprague, plant physiologist at Rutgers University, says, "Drought-resistant plants have a number of common characteristics. They have a short life cycle and a root system that can reach deeply, to gather more water. In addition, they conserve their moisture by transpiring very little."

According to Sprague, when researchers try to develop drought-resistant plants, they start with various strains of a given species. By breeding and crossbreeding, they endeavor:

- to reduce the length of the growing season;
- to increase the length of the taproot or the spread of the root system;
- to decrease the number or size of the stomata in the leaves (stomata are the openings through which water vapor escapes from the leaves to the atmosphere);
- to obtain, in some instances, a waxy coating on the leaves because this too reduces water loss; and

- to boost yield and quality.

High-yield and high-quality drought-resistant crops! Think what these would mean to the world's hungry who live on the semiarid lands of Asia, Africa, and Latin America. If, on their sandy acres, they could cultivate such crops of grain and legumes, they, too, would be able to enjoy the good things of life despite the shortage of fresh water.

Most plant scientists are optimistic and confidently expect more such plants to become available in the future. But some think otherwise. They believe that drought-resistant wheat and rice and sorghum and barley, even drought-resistant legumes such as cowpeas and soybeans, can be developed, but we'll have to settle for poor yield. Not so, say the optimists. They call attention to numerous semiarid regions already planted with drought-resistant hybrid grasses for food and forage. There's the Yemeni Arab Republic, where improved seeds of drought-resistant hybrid sorghum, a cereal grain, produces bountiful harvests. There's the American Southwest, where the new hybrid, *Sorghum bicolor*, has turned out to be a ma-

At harvest time, improved hybrid sorghum stalks are tied together so they won't break under the weight of the cobs. (Food and Agricultural Organization, UN, photo by F. Mattioli)

jor food crop. Here, however, it is used mainly for livestock feed or export, but in many other semiarid countries this grain is ground into high-protein flour for baking. In Africa it is often used in making alcoholic beverages. The optimists also point to the new strains of coastal Bermuda grass that grow tall and fast in relatively dry areas and provide excellent forage for cattle. In this area, the search continues actively.

Plant scientists are also interested in "going mini" and developing dwarf trees that are low-growing and compact. Since such trees can be planted close together, their "population density" is easily increased. Consequently, the available water is utilized more efficiently. The available land is also utilized more efficiently, as is the labor. Today, a number of countries are reporting progress in and profit from their groves of dwarf lemon, apricot, and avocado trees. In this area, research also continues.

When we consider plants and ways of reducing their water requirements, we should also consider the soil, because plants grow in it and because soil is such a great factor in the conservation of moisture. In order to conserve agricultural water, it is necessary to do two things: reduce evaporation from the ground and retain moisture in the ground.

Evaporation from the soil can be prevented by mulching—by spreading straw, hay, leaves, and grass clippings around the growing plants or by laying black plastic sheets between the rows. This is the old-fashioned way of the home gardener, and it works. The soil remains moist beneath its covering, and the plants grow without any extra watering, even after a number of hot summer days.

Within the last few decades, a practice called *no-till* has been gaining favor among agronomists. Till—short for tillage—refers to those things a farmer does to his fields: plowing, disking, and harrowing. When, however, he uses no-till, or minimum till, he disturbs the soil as little as possible. Plowing is out, and so is disking and harrowing. In the spring he simply sprays his fields with a herbicide that kills off the unwanted leftover growth from the previous year. A short time afterward, he rides over the fields on his seeder, which inserts seeds, together with mea-

A no-till field of grain sorghum planted in barley stubble with a fescue grass waterway prevents cascading runoff at the South Piedmont Conservation Research Center. (USDA—ARS photo by W. G. Murray)

Corn growing in wheat stubble on a no-till field at the South Piedmont Conservation Research Center. (Courtesy of Ronald E. Phillips, Professor of Agronomy, University of Kentucky, Lexington 40546)

sured quantities of fertilizer and pesticide, into that un-
tilled field. In due time, the seeds germinate, grow, and
thrive. And they continue to thrive without being stressed
by the loss of water due to evaporation.

In the fall of the year, after the crop is harvested, the
land is left with a natural mulch of whatever residue
there is. So it remains throughout the following winter—
stubbled as a field of grain is stubbled after reaping, or
sodded as a meadow remains sodded after mowing. Come
spring, the process of spraying, seeding, fertilizing, and
adding pesticide is repeated.

The no-till method conserves agricultural water in
yet another way: by preventing runoff from the watershed. After a heavy rain, the farmer who uses conventional agriculture sees the excess water cascading down
the slopes, eroding the soil, gouging gullies, and disap-
pearing into ditches, culverts, and streams. After a similar rain, the farmer who uses no-till agriculture and who,
in addition, has planted a grassed waterway (for example,
of fescue grass in barley stubble) sees no such runoff. The
grassed waterway soaks up the excess raindrops and holds
them until they percolate into the ground.

Clearly, a farmer who practices no or minimum till,
even in semiarid regions, is going to need very little irrigation water. But suppose he has no such fields—only
sandy acres that blow in the wind and act as sieves when
it does rain. Under such conditions, unless he can develop
greenhouse agriculture, he would do well to forget about
those acres.

But one new invention, though not yet economically feasible, offers exciting possibilities for sandy farm
acreage. This is the *super slurper.* In tests around the
country, the super slurper, in flake or powder form, has
stabilized shifting sands and conditioned farm fields.
When added to a potting mix, it increases moisture retention, and the plants consequently require less watering.
When coated on seeds, it absorbs and holds water in a
kind of gel, which results in more efficient germination.

A super slurper flake swells to a chunk that is 99 percent water. It is like a soft, rubbery ice cube that is not cold. (USDA—ARS)

In studies conducted at Iowa University at Ames, when the super slurper was stirred into seed beds, it promoted the growth of oats and other grasses significantly. Actually, you can repeat these tests with a free sample of the slurper from the USDA Agricultural Research Service (ARS) in Peoria, Illinois.

It was at the ARS in Peoria that a team of chemists came up with this "invention," which they named super slurper because they found that 1 pound (.45 kilogram) of it can slurp up—absorb—as much as 2 tons (1.8 metric tons) of water depending on the chemical composition of that water. It is produced by combining starch from corn, wheat, potatoes, or other farm crops with acrylonitrile, a man-made chemical used in the manufacture of acrylic fiber. Cost? About a dollar a pound.

Dr. William M. Doane, member of that team of chemists, says, "If to sandy or any fast-draining soil you add the slurper in a ratio of 1 to 500 (1 part slurper to 500 parts soil), what happens is this. The slurper catches the rain or the irrigation water and releases it slowly to the growing plants. Of course the slurper gets depleted of water as the plants use it up, but the next time it rains or you irrigate, it captures the water again because, you see, the slurper is recyclable."

How long does it last in the soil?

"That we do not yet know," said Dr. Doane. "We have found, however, that after two years of field tests, the soil still shows enhanced water absorption."

Some agronomists are saying that if the slurper is tilled into the top 12 inches (30 centimeters) of a marginal dry field, that field could be converted to productive land. Presently, however, the cost would be too high.

So far, we've been talking of new ways to make every drop of water count. But there are also old, forgotten ways—ancient techniques that once yielded spectacular harvests with little rainfall and no irrigation. Some of these old-time practices are being reconsidered today because they can indeed capture great quantities of water that otherwise would be lost to the sea or to the atmosphere.

One of those old ways was practiced on the Negev Desert, in the tenth century B.C., the time of King Solomon. The Negev has always received only 3 or 4 inches (7.5 or 10 centimeters) of rain a year, and yet it used to produce bountiful grain crops for export.

How was this possible?

Dr. Michael Evanari rolled back the centuries and discovered the answer. Evanari, a professor at the Institute for Desert Research, Sede Boqer, at the Ben Gurion University of the Negev, in Israel, solved the puzzle, which turns out to be no puzzle at all. It is simply a matter of harvesting what little water there is in the desert. As he explains it, the water source was not the rain that fell on the Negev Highlands but the runoff that streamed down the hillsides. This runoff amounted to about 25 percent of the rainfall, but by channeling it into catchment areas, the farmers were able to catch 1 inch (2.5 centimeters) of water (25 percent of 4 inches equals 1 inch.) If, as was usually the case, the catchment area was 30 times as large as the farm, that farm had at its disposal 30 inches (76 centimeters) of rain! And with 30 inches of rain, who needed irrigation?

Today, Evanari successfully manages such a desert farm at Avdat, where he raises almond and pistachio trees, pasture grass for sheep, and vegetables for seed. Other countries are also reporting successful management of such desert farms. They are in Afghanistan, Pakistan, India, Niger, Kenya, Mexico, Australia, and Upper Volta.

Ideas for the best possible utilization of every drop of water invariably come from lands where water is scarce. So we note again that Israel, ever in need of water, has found *dew* to be a good source.

By definition, dew is moisture that condenses from

the atmosphere onto cool surfaces as the temperature drops. Dew accumulates most heavily on cloudless nights. Dew? Is there actually enough of it to contribute to the growth of plants?

Dr. S. Duvedani found that it did. Working on the semiarid coastal plain where heavy nightly dews occur frequently, he compared two field plots of plants. Both plots were treated identically except that, throughout the growing season, one was covered with a canopy between sunset and sunrise to prevent the possibility of dew formation. The other plot was not covered. Duvedani found that the uncovered plot, the one that received its nightly dew, produced squash and corn twice the size of the squash and corn from the covered plot.

Countless field observations in semiarid regions have indicated again and again that dew is indeed a source of water that keeps plants growing. In some forsaken areas, such as parts of southern California, annual plants—the wild buckwheat and some gilias, to name just two—thrive well and manage to keep green and growing for months after the last rain. Because these plants have small, restricted root systems that cannot reach out for underground waters, the investigators conclude that moisture for such plants must come from atmospheric condensation, which in this instance means dew.

On Lanzarote, one of the Spanish Islands in the Canary chain, it is dew that enables the people to produce and enjoy their very excellent, strong, sweet Malvasia wine. On that bone-dry volcanic island, which is sparsely inhabited by people and camels, rain falls perhaps seven times a year. The terrain resembles a rough, black cindery moonscape, yet grapevines flourish magnificently. Set in cuplike pits each about 3 feet (1 meter) in diameter and 3 feet in depth, each vine thrives without any irrigation at all. The black cindery rocks heat up fiercely during the day, cool quickly at nightfall, then get coated with dew that drains into the pit. At the same time dew drenches the leaves, stems, and roots of the vines. Walking through those dry Lanzarote vineyards, one can only marvel at the way nature provides.

In a dripping redwood forest in northern California, however, *fog* is the factor, not dew. There, as the daily fogs drift in from the Pacific, droplets condense on the leaves and branches of the redwoods. When the droplets grow large enough, they drip.

Another example of fog serving as a natural source of water can be seen in southern California, on an arid coastal strip where farmers raise abundant crops of tomatoes, peppers, beans, and other vegetables. With no water supplied by the farmers and no rain falling between May and October, the plants grow vigorously, their water requirements filled only by the fog. In other arid regions, clever growers make a practice of sowing their seeds and then waiting for the fog to roll in. When it does, they quickly cover the plants with branches. The fog condenses on the branches and collects in great droplets, which drip down and water the planting. Good yields are reported without benefit of irrigation. Elsewhere, in Chile, to be exact, farmers set nylon screens to intercept the fog and extract water drops from it. Although these are what you might call primitive methods, they work, and the proof is in the fine crops they support.

Most of us are familiar with the fogs that drift in now and then, only to blow away and be gone. But in some areas, there are perpetual fogs. These are called *fog deserts*, a misnomer if ever there was one because they supply such an abundance of moisture to the plants.

Fog deserts can be found along the coasts of southwest Africa and Peru in arid regions that border the sea and are backed by mountains. As the dry heated air rises against the mountains, atmospheric vapor condenses, and extensive fogs form at an altitude of 1,000 feet (305 meters). There the fogs hang, and there, 1,000 feet above the dry and barren mountainsides, you can see a positive explosion of water-loving trees, shrubs, plants, and air plants climbing over one another and over the mosses that thicken the branches.

These are nonconventional albeit natural sources of water we've been talking about, but much research is needed before farmers can significantly increase the deposition of moisture from fog and dew.

Making every drop of water count by technological and biological means spells high-level water management. Add to that the increasingly successful projects-in-progress—to conserve irrigation water through improved agricultural practices, to convert seawater and brine deposits to fresh, to seed rain clouds for precipitation enhancement, to reclaim waste water for replenishing aquifers, to provide utility water for dual systems, and to treat water supplies for safety—and clearly there is no need to be unduly worried about the planet's fresh-water supplies in the future.

As Maurice Maeterlinck observed, "The Future is a world limited only by ourselves . . ."

And as Alfred Lord Tennyson put it,

"For I dipt into the future, far as human eye could see,
Saw the Vision of the world, and all the wonder that
    would be."

To those who still say, "Yes, but . . ." who still worry and wail about the world's water because sometimes there's too much, sometimes there's too little, and between times it's too polluted, to those one can only say, "Look. Look and see. The answers are all around you."

ACKNOWLEDGMENTS

Scores of people, ranging from country well diggers to flying cloud seeders, from water scientists to desert ecologists and flood control engineers, have helped in the preparation of this book. They sent me invaluable data and maps, photographs, slides, and water samples. In personal interviews, telephone conversations, and lively, informative letters, they encouraged the work.

For critiquing the entire manuscript and offering invaluable assistance, my very special thanks go to: Dr. Martin G. Beyer, UNICEF; Dr. F. Eugene McJunkin, Office of Health, Agency for International Development; and Dr. Daniel A. Okun, University of North Carolina.

With no less appreciation, I recognize the following, who read one or more chapters and offered constructive criticism: Dr. Saul Arlosoroff, World Bank; Dr. Jacob Avni, Embassy of Israel; Dr. Joseph Barnea, United Nations Institute for Training and Research; Gordon Elser and Lola Handy, Water Factory 21, Bureau of Reclamation, U.S. Department of the Interior; Hélène Gosselin, UNICEF; Jesse Haffen, the Town of Newburgh Filtration Plant; Wilfred S. Hahn, Office of Water Research and Technology, U.S. Department of the Interior; Dr. Gary Margheim, U.S. Department of Agriculture, Soil Conservation Service; Dr. Octave Levenspiel, University of Oregon at Corvallis;

James R. Melton, Santa Clara Valley Water District, California; Dr. Richard F. Meyer, Julian Soren, and Dr. George C. Taylor, Jr. (retired), U.S. Geological Survey; Dr. Bernard Silverman and Linda Woodworth, Office of Atmospheric Resources Research, Bureau of Reclamation, U.S. Department of the Interior; Edward F. Wehlage, International Society for Geothermal Engineers; Mary C. Woods, *California Geology.*

Warm thanks, too, go to these new-found friends who read selected pages within their particular fields of expertise: Dr. Rolf Bettaque, Federal Republic of Germany; Dr. James R. Crook, Department of Health Services, California; Dr. William Doane, Agricultural Research Service, U.S. Department of Agriculture; Dr. Emanuel Epstein, University of California at Davis; Dr. Elias Fereres, Extension Division, University of California at Davis; Lawrence Goodrich, the Town of Newburgh Filtration Plant; Dr. James R. Jones and Neal E. McClymonds, U.S. Geological Survey; Dr. Jack Keller, Utah State University; Arthur Kuhn, Land Leveling, Inc., Brawley, California; Bill Montana, Imperial Irrigation District at Imperial Dam, California; Julian Rhinehart and Bob Walsh, Lower Colorado Region Office, Bureau of Reclamation, U.S. Department of the Interior; Dr. Milton A. Sprague, Rutgers University.

And much gratitude goes to these kindly professionals who provided additional direction, materials, and graphics: Arik Arazi, Consulate General of Israel; Dr. Morris J. Bitzer, Extension Division, University of Kentucky; Bueford L. Bradley, Imperial Irrigation District, California; Jim Breetveld and Anthony Hewitt, UNICEF; Peter G. Bourne, M.D., and Hilda Pacqui, United Nations Development Programme, International Drinking Water Supply and Sanitation Decade; Mrs. J. C. David, National Oceanic and Atmospheric Administration, U.S. Department of Commerce; Harold Donahue and Michael L. Scalf, TVA; John Donovan, Camp Dresser and McKee, Inc.; Dr. Harold Dregne, Dr. Joseph Goodin, and Dr. Idris Rhea Traylor, International Center for Arid and Semi Arid Land Studies; John Goerg, New York State Department of Environmental Conservation; Lila Goldin, Food and Agricultural Organization; Eugene Herzog, Eugene Hinds, Raymond A. Jensen, Dr. Archie M. Kahan, Robert Pauline, Bureau of Reclamation, U.S. Department of the Interior; Dr. T. B. Kinney, Jr., Dr. G. W. Langdale, Dr. Eugene V. Maas, and Anita Y. Rogers, Agricultural Research Service, U.S. Department of Agriculture; Jody Kurty and Thomas W. Levermann, U.S. Department of Agriculture, Soil Conservation Service; Dr. Frank Kreith, Solar Energy Research Institute; Dorothy Lathrop and Dr. Raymond L. Nace, Retired, U.S. Geological Survey; Norman Longmate, author; Dr. Werner Luft, International Solar Energy Institute; Dr. George C. Marks and David Myers, Soil Conservation Service, Texas; Dr. William M. Mesner, Extension Division, University of Kentucky; John Metelsky, Agency for International Development; Dr. Ronald E. Phillips, University of Kentucky; Richard Taylor and Becky Perez, Community and Special Services, Imperial Irrigation District, California; Gordon H. Tenney, State of Utah Natural Resources.

If I have inadvertently omitted the names of any persons who helped me, my sincere apologies. If there are any errors in these pages, the fault is mine alone.

BIBLIOGRAPHY

Books

Babbitt, Harold E.; Doland, James J.; and Cleasby, John L. *Water Supply Engineering.* New York: McGraw-Hill, 1967.

Baker, M. N. *The Quest for Pure Water.* New York: The American Waterworks Association, 1949.

Biswas, Asit K. *History of Hydrology.* New York: American Elsevier Publishing Company, 1970.

Carlson, Carl Walter, and Carlson, Berice Wells. *Water Fit to Use.* New York: John Day, 1966.

Carter, Vernon Gill, and Dale, Tom. *Topsoil and Civilization.* Norman, Oklahoma: University of Oklahoma Press, 1974.

Deming, H. G. *Water.* New York: Oxford University Press, 1975.

Donovan, John; Bates, John E.; and Rowell, Clark H. *Guidelines for Water Reuse.* Boston: Camp Dresser and McKee, 1980.

Draffin, Jasper Owen. *The Story of Man's Quest for Water.* Champaign, Illinois: Garrard Press, 1939.

Falkenmark, Malin, and Lindh, Gunmar. *Water for a Starving World.* Boulder, Colorado: Westview Press, 1976.

Gibson, Ulric P., and Singer, Rexford D. *Water Well Manual.* Berkeley, California: Premier Press, 1971.

Goldin, Augusta. *Grass: The Everything, Everywhere Plant.* New York: Thomas Nelson, 1977.

Hess, W. N. *Weather and Climate Modification.* New York: John Wiley and Sons, 1974.

Leopold, Luna B.; Davis, Kenneth S.; and the Editors of *Life. Water.* New York: Time, 1966.

Longmate, Norman. *King Cholera, The Biography of a Disease.* London: Hamish Hamilton, 1966.

McJunkin, Frederick Eugene. *Water, Engineers, Development, and Disease in the Tropics.* Washington, D.C.: Agency for International Development, 1975.

McArthur, Seonaid, and Melton, James, R., eds. *Water in the Santa Clara Valley: A History.* Cupertino, California: California History Center, 1981.

Mussell, Harry, and Staples, Richard C. *Stress Physiology in Crop Plants.* New York: John Wiley and Sons, 1979.

Okun, Daniel A. *Regionalization of Water Management: A Revolution in England and Wales.* England: Applied Science Publishers, 1977.

Phillips, R. E.; Thomas, G. W.; and Blevins, R. L., eds. *No-Tillage Research: Research Reports and Reviews.* Lexington, Kentucky: University of Kentucky, College of Agriculture and Agricultural Experiment Station, 1981.

Saunders, Robert J., and Warford, Jeremy J. *Village Water Supply—Economics and Policy in the Developing World.* Baltimore and London: Johns Hopkins University Press, 1976.

Talsma, T., and Philip, J. R., eds. *Salinity and Water Use.* New York: John Wiley and Sons, 1971.

Water, the Yearbook of Agriculture. Washington, D.C.: The United States Department of Agriculture, 1955.

United States Government Publications

The A-B-C of Desalting. Office of Water Research and Technology Transfer, U.S. Department of the Interior, 1977.

America's Soil and Water: Conditions and Trends. Soil Conservation Service, U.S. Department of Agriculture, 1980.

Baldwin, H. L., and McGuiness, C. L. *A Primer on Ground Water.* Geological Survey, U.S. Department of the Interior, 1976.

Before the Well Runs Dry. Geological Survey, U.S. Department of the Interior, 1981.

Bernstein, Leon. *Salt Tolerance of Vegetable Crops in the West.* Agricultural Research Service, U.S. Department of Agriculture, 1959.

Davis, Joseph A., ed. *Groundwater Protection.* Water Planning Division, U.S. Environmental Protection Agency, 1980.

Electrodialysis Technology. Office of Water Research and Technology, U.S. Department of the Interior, 1979.

Feth, J. H. *Water Facts and Figures for Planners and Managers.* Geological Survey, U.S. Department of the Interior, 1973.

Gallatin, M. H.; Lunin, J.; and Batchelder, A. R. *Brackish Water Sources for Irrigation along the Eastern Seaboard of the United States.* Agricultural Research Service, U.S. Department of Agriculture, 1962.

The Global 2000 Report. The U.S. Government Printing Office for the Council on Environmental Quality and the U.S. Department of State, 1980.

Laska, Richard. *Acid Rain.* Office of Research and Development, U.S. Environmental Protection Agency, 1980.

Leopold, Luna B. *The Challenge of Water Management.* Geological Survey, U.S. Department of the Interior, 1967.

Leopold, Luna B., and Langbein, Walter B. *A Primer on Water.* Geological Survey, U.S. Department of the Interior, 1970.

McClymonds, Neal E. *Shallow Groundwater in the Zamin Dawar Area, Afghanistan.* The U.S. Geological Survey in cooperation with the Government of Afghanistan under the auspices of the Agency for International Development, 1972.

The Nation's Water Resources 1975–2000, Vol. 1: Summary. U.S. Water Resources Council, U.S. Government Office, 1979.

215

New Water. Office of Saline Water, U.S. Department of the Interior, 1970.

Project Skywater. Bureau of Reclamation, U.S. Department of the Interior, 1961.

Project Skywater, Fiscal Year 1979 Report. Atmospheric Research Program, U.S. Department of the Interior, 1981.

Reverse Osmosis. Office of Water Research and Technology, U.S. Department of the Interior, 1979.

Swenson, H. A., and Baldwin, H. L. *A Primer on Water Quality.* Geological Survey, U.S. Department of the Interior, 1973.

Water Factory 21. Office of Water Research and Technology, U.S. Department of the Interior, 1978.

Articles

Ambroggi, Robert P. "Underground Reservoirs to Control the Water Cycle." *Scientific American,* Vol. 236, No. 5 (May 1977), pp. 21–27.

———. "Water." *Scientific American,* Vol. 243, No. 3 (September 1980), pp. 100–116.

Arlosoroff, Saul. "Water Resource Development and Management in Israel." *Kidma,* Vol. 3, No. 2 (November 1977), pp. 4–10.

Beyer, Martin J. "Making Children's Lives More Liveable." *UNICEF News,* Issue 103, No. 1 (1980/1), pp. 3–6.

Epstein, Emanuel, and Norlyn, J. D. "Seawater-Based Crop Production: A Feasibility Study." *Science,* Vol. 197, No. 4300 (July 1977), pp. 249–251.

Howell, Wallace E. "Environmental Impacts of Precipitation Management: Results and Inferences from Project Skywater." *The Bulletin of the American Meteorological Society,* Vol. 58, No. 6 (June 1977), pp. 488–501.

Hughes, Helen R. "The Mighty Waikato." *Soil and Water,* Vol. 16, No. 2 (April 1980), pp. 6–9.

Jones, James R. "Groundwater Development in Libya." *Water Well Journal,* February 1966.

Keller, Jack, and Karmeli, David. "Trickle Irrigation Design Parameters." *Transactions*, Vol. 17, No. 4 (January 1974), pp. 679–684.

Langdale, G. W.; Barnett, A. P.; Leonard, R. A.; and Fleming, W. G. "Reduction of Soil Erosion by the No-Till System." *Transactions*, Vol. 22, No. 1 (1979), pp. 82–86 and 92.

Okun, Daniel A. "A Water Quality Hierarchy for Arid Lands." *Arid Lands in Perspective*, 1969, pp. 291–296.

Pillsbury, Arthur F. "The Salinity of Rivers." *Scientific American*, Vol. 245, No. 1 (July 1981), pp. 54–65.

Shoji, Kobe. "Drip Irrigation." *Scientific American*, Vol. 237, No. 5 (November 1977), pp. 62–68.

Silverman, Bernard A. "What Do We Need in Weather Modification?" *Journal of Applied Meteorology*, Vol. 17, No. 6 (June 1978), pp. 867–871.

Taylor, George C., Jr. "The United Nations Groundwater Exploration and Development Programme—a Fifteen-Year Perspective." *Natural Resources Forum 3*, 1979, pp. 147–166.

Papers, Talks, Proceedings

Bettaque, Rolf. "Eco Islands in Arid Zones." In *Proceedings of the 6th International Symposium on Fresh Water from the Sea*, Gran Canaria, Spain, September 17–22, 1978, pp. 23–28.

Bourne, Peter G., M.D. "The United Nations International Drinking Water Supply and Sanitation Decade." Presented at the 13th Congress of the International Water Supply Association, Paris, France, September 1, 1980.

Doane, William M. "Starch: Renewable Raw Material for the Chemical Industry." Presented at the Annual Meeting of the Philadelphia Society for Coatings Technology, Mount Laurel, New Jersey, May 2, 1977.

Dregne, Harold E. "Desertification: Causes, Effects, and Assessment." Seminar on Remote Sensing Applications and Technology Transfer for International Development, Ann Arbor, Michigan, April 18–21, 1979.

Elmendorf, Mary. "Women, Water, and Waste: Beyond Access." Mid-Decade Forum, World Conference of the United Nations Decade for Women, Copenhagen, Denmark, July 1980.

Kahan, Archie M. "Weather Modification—Past, Present and Future." Presented at the 49th Annual Convention of the Association of Western State Engineers, Topeka, Kansas, September 21–22, 1976.

Kreith, Frank, and Luft, Werner. "An Overview of Solar Desalination Technologies." Solar Energy Research Institute, Golden, Colorado, 1981.

Luft, Werner. "Solar Energy Water Desalination in the United States and Saudi Arabia." Ninth Annual Conference and International Trade Fair: Water and Energy for the 80s, Washington, D.C., May 31–June 4, 1981.

Maas, E. V., and Hoffman, G. J. "Crop Salt Tolerance—Current Assessment." Presented at the ASCE Irrigation and Drainage Division Specialty Conference, Logan, Utah, August 13–15, 1975.

Okun, Daniel A. "New Approaches in Water Supply and Sanitation for Developing Countries." Presented at a short course at the University of Ottawa, Canada, June 22–25, 1981.

"Weather Modification Programme, Precipitation Enhancement Project, Report No. 25." World Meteorological Organization, Geneva, Switzerland, May 1981.

"Report of the Eleventh Session of the Experts on Weather Modification." World Meteorological Organization, Geneva, Switzerland, May 11–16, 1981.

Schaefer, Vincent J. "The Serendipitous Happenings which Led to Weather Modification." Atmospheric Sciences Research Center, State University of New York, 1981.

Silverman, Bernard A. "The Scientific Basis for Seeding Summer and Wintertime Clouds." Broadcast over the Montana Educational Network, Miles City, Montana, Jan. 30, 1981.

Sprague, Milton A. "Stepping Stones to Better Tillage for a Permanent Agriculture." Presented at the Eastern Branch Meeting, American Society of Agronomy, Rutgers University, New Brunswick, New Jersey, June 26, 1979.

218

Bulletins, Brochures, Reports

Decade Briefing, The International Drinking Water Supply and Sanitation Decade 1981–1990. United Nations Development Programme, 1981.

Decade Dossier, The International Drinking Water Supply and Sanitation Decade 1981–1990. United Nations Development Programme in collaboration with UNICEF and WHO, 1981.

Evanari, Michael. *The Desert Ecosystem Programme.* The Institute of Desert Research, Sede Boqer, Ben Gurion University of the Negev, 1980.

Fereres, Elias, ed. *Drip Irrigation and Management.* Division of Agricultural Sciences, University of California at Berkeley, 1981.

Melton, James R., ed. *The Story of the Santa Clara Valley Water District.* Santa Clara Valley Water District, 1978.

Rural Water Supply Handpumps Project, Report No. 1. United Nations Development Programme and World Bank. Washington, D.C., March 1982.

INDEX

Page numbers in italics refer to illustrations